Dispute Avoidance

A non-confrontational approach to the management of construction contracts

Dispute Avoidance

A non-confrontational approach to the management of construction contracts

D. Bryan Morgan

RIBA ∰ **Publishing**

© D. Bryan Morgan, 2008

Published by RIBA Publishing, 15 Bonhill Street, London EC2P 2EA

ISBN 978 1 85946 297 3

Stock Code 64212

The right of D. Bryan Morgan to be identified as the Author of this Work has been asserted in accordance with the Copyright, Design and Patents Act 1988.

British Library Cataloguing in Publication Data
A catalogue record for this book is available from the British Library.

Publisher: Steven Cross

Commissioning Editor: Matthew Thompson

Project Editor: 4word Ltd, Bristol

Designed by Ben Millbank

Typeset by 4word Ltd, Bristol

Printed and bound by MPG Books Ltd, Bodmin, Cornwall

While every effort has been made to check the accuracy of the information given in this book, readers should always make their own checks. Neither the Author nor the Publisher accept any responsibility for misstatements made in it or misunderstandings arising from it.

RIBA Publishing is part of RIBA Enterprises Ltd www.ribaenterprises.com

Contents

Contents

Preface

My first book, *International Construction Contract Management*, gave a broad overview of construction management from a largely international perspective. It touched briefly on contractual claims and discussed in some detail the various aspects of contract administration under a number of individual headings. In addition, it explained briefly the different approaches to construction management taken in different parts of the world, the methods employed and the various terms used.

This second book assumes that the reader is versed in basic contract administration, and will demonstrate how those skills can be used and developed further so that disputes can be avoided, or at least managed effectively. It will help the reader to understand the various kinds of dispute, the circumstances under which one can arise, and the measures that can be taken in order to prevent minor disagreements developing into major disputes that by their very nature are only resolvable by one of the recognised systems of alternative dispute resolution (ADR), arbitration or litigation. It will help the reader to understand the different approaches to resolving disputes before they reach the stage where formal ADR, arbitration or litigation procedures have to be initiated.

There is a significant and often misunderstood difference between disputes and claims under a contract. Claims can be a legitimate means of recouping both additional time and additional costs expended by a party to a contract due to some reason or reasons not attributable to the claimant, and are usually made in accordance with provisions included within the terms and conditions of the contract. It is suggested that 'claims' should in fact be referred to as 'contractual entitlements'; if they were then the disassociation of the words 'claims' and 'disputes' would result in significant savings in the time, effort and money currently expended fighting claims. At the moment the very mention of the word 'claim' immediately gives rise to fears of disputes, formal proceedings, lawyers and costs. This should not be the case.

If one party is asking another party to grant it an entitlement provided for by one of the clauses in the contract, there should be no grounds for dispute, unless of course the request is being made erroneously or is based on false facts. Only then should the entitlement become a contentious issue which could, if not dealt with in the proper manner, develop into a dispute, at which point one of the dispute resolution mechanisms included in the contract for use in such situations would be called on to ascertain a judgment on the relative merits of the opposing party's assertions.

If a contract is managed effectively, if the parties to the contract develop a good working relationship, if clear, concise, contemporaneous records are maintained and clear channels of communication are implemented from the beginning of the project through to its completion, then the likelihood of disputes arising should be minimised. If any disputes do arise they will be much easier to settle if there are good records of contemporaneous and prior communications between the parties concerning the issue in dispute. It is far better to spend time identifying and discussing a potentially problematic situation or event in an amicable manner on a one-to-one basis than to react immediately with confrontational contractual correspondence or call hasty meetings where each party immediately establishes a corner from which it will find it harder to move as the dispute develops, as it inevitably will in such a scenario.

Dispute avoidance is not about preventing issue-based disagreements, nor is it about parties keeping silent if they disagree on a particular issue. It is about reducing the potential for a dispute to develop as a result of misunderstandings, misconceptions, miscommunication and particular behavioural patterns. It is largely about learning how to say things in ways, and using words, that do not immediately rile the other party. Body language, choice of words, tone and phrasing of communication are all tools in the process of resolving potentially contentious issues; however, if these tools are misused a dispute can escalate out of all proportion.

The application of the information and guidance given in this book has no boundaries and will be of benefit to practitioners of every construction-related discipline whatever country they are working in and under whatever formal contract their project has been procured. The application of the advice given is not restricted to this or any other year and will hopefully be as pertinent in twenty years as it is when this book was published. It does not relate to judicial precedents, laws and regulations in force at a given time, nor does it depend upon whether the relevant jurisdiction is based on common or civil law.

Much of the information and guidance proffered in this book has been accumulated during, and developed from, my fourty-five years of practical experience. Seasoned professionals will hopefully discover in this book items they had not previously considered or fully appreciated, and in addition students, recent graduates and others in the relatively early stages of their career, and to whom a contractual dispute is a nebulous event they have heard about in the course of their studies or their introduction to management but have not yet experienced, will also benefit from its study. The content is equally relevant to contractors, surveyors, architects, developers and, in fact, to anyone involved in business relationships of any kind; it is not necessarily limited to the construction industry. Where references are made in this book to an 'employer' this can, in a construction project context, be understood as applying equally to the architect or engineer engaged by the employer, since these are the people who will in all probability be carrying out the day-to-day management of the project on its behalf.

Introduction to dispute management

1

1.1 DEFINITIONS AND CORE CONCEPTS

1.1.1 Definition of dispute, dispute avoidance and dispute management

There is a school of thought that defines a dispute as a short-term disagreement that is relatively easy to resolve, and defines a conflict as a deep-rooted problem involving seemingly non-negotiable issues resistant to resolution. Other definitions state that conflict exists if the parties have opposing interests, values or needs, and this can be either latent (not acted upon) or manifest, in which case it takes shape as a dispute.

For the purposes of this book the word 'dispute' has been taken to apply to all contentious issues that the parties to a construction contract disagree upon, or would be likely to disagree upon, and which need to be resolved by some means or other either within or outside the contract. No distinction has been made between disputes and conflicts, and references to a dispute should be taken as applying similarly to a conflict. This book assumes that a dispute arises when an issue that is in contention fails to be resolved by open discussions between the parties, or by mutual application by the parties of the terms and conditions of the contract they have entered into. A state of contention is considered for the purposes of this book to be a predecessor of a dispute, and is not in itself considered a dispute.

The intention of this book is to show how it is possible to reduce the number of disputes that are likely to occur on a construction project and to show how they can be managed and overcome should they arise. Two parties may have a difference of opinion over the true value of a piece of equipment or over the time necessary to execute a particular piece of work, but eventually, by a process of negotiation and compromise, a solution acceptable to both can usually be agreed upon. Disputes are primarily concerned with contentious issues that are negotiable or for which solutions should be available. This book will concentrate on identifying and overcoming those contentions before the issues become disputes, and on overcoming any disputes that may arise in the simplest, quickest and least confrontational manner possible.

Dispute avoidance is in reality nothing more than a blend of good commercial and project management. The personnel responsible for the project's execution must be blessed with good interpersonal and diplomatic skills over and above their commercial and technical skills in order to carry out their tasks effectively. Dispute avoidance involves the proper use of all the tools available to the project team, including principally the Terms and Conditions of Contract and the Contract Schedule. If these are applied correctly then the chances of avoiding a dispute are considerably greater than if they are ignored or merely paid lip service to.

1

Dispute management comes into play when dispute avoidance has in effect failed, and requires exceptional diplomacy and negotiation skills over and above those employed in traditional commercial and project management. Dispute management must be based upon a well thought out strategy. A mistake frequently made by those unfamiliar with the finer points of dispute management is that it can merely happen, which can lead to frustration, confusion and an escalation of the disputes in hand. If there is no defined strategy then there is a significant likelihood that initial disputes will spawn further disputes, and the whole process will become more complex and less likely to result in a settlement.

Those involved in dispute management must establish, or be presented by higher management with, the goals that they hope to achieve before proceeding. With these goals the dispute management team is able to prepare a strategy to which it must adhere as closely as possible. While there is a desire to achieve certain goals, there is a clear understanding that there will need to be an element of give and take by both parties. In other words, the dispute management team must approach the agreed strategy with a degree of flexibility.

The goals should be graded such that the dispute management team knows what the ideal goal is and what the 'bottom line' is, i.e. what is the least result that higher management would be prepared to accept as a viable solution to the dispute. A bottom line acts as a final barrier beyond which the negotiator must not pass. Alternatively, the dispute management team may identify its BATNA (best alternative to negotiated agreement). This differs from a bottom line in that it can be brought into play earlier. A BATNA determines the course of action to be taken if a negotiated agreement is not reached within a certain period. It prevents a negotiator accepting an unfavourable agreement by providing a better option outside the negotiation. If that fails then the negotiation can recommence until the bottom line comes into play.

The dispute management process lasts from the time the contentious issue is recognised until the goals set by the dispute management team or higher management have been achieved. How this actually works will depend upon the nature of the dispute, but will always be directed at maximising the benefits to the party managing the dispute, whether that is the employer (or the architect acting on its behalf), contractor, subcontractor or consultant. These benefits can be principally commercial (finance or time related) or technical (design, manufacture, supply or installation/construction related), or a combination of both.

The dispute management team must identify where the dispute lies in the context of the contract terms and conditions, including the technical specifications, drawings and other documents. The team must establish its strengths and weaknesses under the contract and plan accordingly. If it perceives that its contractual position is strong then it will be able to adopt a robust negotiating stance. If weak then its approach must be more conciliatory and the team members' interpersonal skills will be tested to the full.

Parties on weak ground often try to bluff their way through by adopting an aggressive approach. This is not to be recommended. The weak ground will eventually be exposed, particularly if the dispute ends up being referred to one of the alternative dispute resolution (ADR) procedures, by which stage the team's chances of reaching an acceptable settlement may well have been adversely compromised by the team's initial aggressive approach.

Overall, dispute management must be centred upon a desire to avoid unnecessary escalation of a dispute and to reach a settlement which is acceptable to all parties, which sits comfortably within the constraints of the contract and which causes the minimum amount of delay and disruption to the contract works.

1.1.2 Core concepts

It is generally accepted that attitudes influence behaviour and that such influence is affected by various moderating factors. Attitude in this context has been described as 'a positive or negative feeling toward a person or object'.[1] The way in which a dispute is dealt with will depend largely on the positive or negative feeling with which it is viewed initially and the moderating factors that are applied.

Communication is critical in avoiding disputes and depends on the parties' desire to prevent a dispute arising, their willingness to communicate and the right environment for such communication to take place. Communication is not merely about holding meetings or writing letters; it is about regular interaction between the parties' representatives, at all levels, allowing them to feel comfortable to express their opinions freely while listening to the other party in an active and focused manner. The combination of clarity of expression and active listening encourages an atmosphere of positive cooperation.

Figure 1 indicates the different behavioural styles adopted in dispute situations and the focus messages those styles send to the other party as to how the dispute is, or is likely to be, approached by that party. The most acceptable approach is obviously the problem-solving approach as that is more likely to bring the parties together in the cooperative spirit necessary to either avoid or resolve the dispute. The competition approach will inevitably escalate the dispute through polarisation of views. The avoidance approach will serve no useful purpose in the long run; the dispute is unlikely to go away of its own accord, and the longer it is left the harder it will be to reach a mutually acceptable solution. The project team should be directed by higher management as to which approach is to be adopted, otherwise its approach may be adversely affected by its members' behavioural patterns, general attitudes to other parties to the contract, specific feelings towards the other party

Fig. 1 Analysis of Behavioural Styles

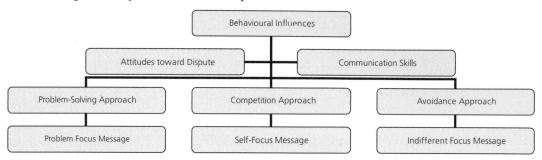

in the dispute and their own communication skills.

The core concepts applicable to the opposing parties in dispute situations are:

a. the conceptions they have of each other and the attitudes with which they approach the dispute;

b. the grievances they hold against each other;

c. the goals they set to change the effect and nature of their grievances; and

d. the means used to achieve their goals, in particular the level of communication skills employed in the avoidance or resolution of a dispute.

A common factor that has particular relevance to the way in which each of these four core concepts influences how the dispute is resolved is the basic approach of the respective parties to the dispute. We can identify five different approaches that may be used:

*   'win–lose' concept – short-term adversarial approach;

*   'win–win' concept – integrative, cooperative approach;

*   'lose–lose' concept;

*   long-term approach;

*   power strategy mix approach.

These different approaches will now be explored in more detail.

1.1.2.1 'Win–lose'

In a win–lose situation one party is prepared to win at all costs and does not particularly care about the other party's interests. One party will walk away from the dispute acknowledging that it has lost, while the other will be content in the knowledge that it has won. This does not help cement relationships between the parties and is not the best solution where that relationship is to continue or where it had scope for developing into a far more significant relationship. A win–lose solution may be inevitable due to the facts of the case. In this situation the issues in question should not have been allowed to reach such a heightened dispute stage. Dispute avoidance techniques should have been employed once the contentious issue was identified and measures should have been taken to ensure that the issue did not escalate into a dispute. The most commendable approach in such a situation would be to take all possible steps to reach an amicable solution at the earliest opportunity, possibly involving some element of compromise, so that neither party felt that it had in fact lost.

1.1.2.2 'Win–win'

The win–win solution is one where both parties feel positive about the way in which the negotiations progressed and each considers that they can benefit in some way. Apart from the tangible benefits of the achieved solution, the win–win approach helps the parties maintain a good working relationship. In order to reach a win–win situation the parties need to:

- see the problems from the other party's point of view in terms of the needs and concerns of the other party;
- identify the key issues and concerns (as opposed to positions) involved;
- determine what results would make a fully acceptable solution;
- identify new options that would facilitate the achievement of those results.

The options would in all probability involve a trade-off, in which case party 'A' must desire what party 'B' is prepared to trade and party 'B' must be prepared to accommodate those desires. If trade is not possible then the party giving way in the negotiations must receive something in the form of compensation for doing so. Ultimately both sides should feel comfortable with the final outcome if the agreement is to be considered win–win.

1.1.2.3 'Lose–lose'

A lose–lose situation can occur when one party becomes obsessed with making the other party lose at all costs, and common sense and reason are ignored. The issue in dispute has become more of a personal grievance than a question of fact, and the aggrieved party will spare no expense in making the other party suffer, irrespective of the value, financial or otherwise, of the dispute. The aggrieved party will disregard the original aim of the negotiations, which in all probability was to benefit them in some way, or at the very least to maintain a state of equilibrium, and will be prepared to suffer a loss so long as its opponent is made to suffer. This is not the point of dispute avoidance or of the negotiation process.

1.1.2.4 Long-term approach

Where the parties are contemplating a long-term relationship between their various business interests their negotiations should be tempered accordingly. If that relationship is already benefiting from having been in place for some time then the likelihood of reaching an amicable settlement is greater than would be the case if the parties were new to each other and had not yet had the opportunity to establish such a close relationship. It is unlikely that parties contemplating a long-term relationship would settle for anything less than a win–win solution; to do so would undermine their long-term intentions. Whatever solution they reach will ultimately set a precedent for dealing with any future issues which have the potential to escalate into disputes.

1.1.2.5 Power strategy mix approach

In a power strategy mix, elements of 'force' are mixed with persuasion in order to reach a settlement. This often occurs where one party has superior bargaining power to the other, such as a major international contractor in dispute with a small local subcontractor. The dominant party should not use its power in such a way, but inevitably this does happen. This approach to dispute avoidance or settlement will lead to the party with the lesser bargaining power feeling aggrieved by the result, and therefore less likely to contribute meaningfully to any ongoing relationship with the dominant party.

In order to determine the most advantageous power mix it is useful to allocate each of the parties to one of four groups:

- Persuadables – those who can be persuaded fairly easily using a little bit of reasoning that the other party's opinion is more likely to be the correct one.

- Reluctant persuadables – those who might be persuaded to support the other party's opinion but will require a little more effort to be expended.

- Traders – those who will not be persuaded but who are prepared to negotiate in any case. They may agree to give the other party what it wants in return for getting something that they want in return, even if they do not agree that the other party is right.

- Extremists – those who are not going to change their opinions whatever the other party says or does. Persuasion will not work on extremists, nor will extremists work on an exchange basis as traders would. They refuse to negotiate whatever is offered.

Different strategies are required for each of these groups. Persuadables should be approached with logical arguments and facts supporting the other party's opinion. Reluctant persuadables need a little more in the way of hard evidence supporting that opinion, possibly backed up by independent reports commissioned specifically in respect of the issues in contention. Traders respond to negotiation based on cooperative and integrative strategies. Extremists are rare in the context of construction disputes, and disputes in which they are involved will invariably end up being referred to one of the ADR systems or to arbitration.

1.2 STAGES IN A DISPUTE

1.2.1 Latent and emerging

A latent dispute can arise at the start of a contractual relationship or at any time during its currency. It occurs when one of the parties recognises that it has issues that bother it but which are not significant enough at the time to cause the party to raise them officially with the other party.

A latent dispute becomes an emerging dispute when a trigger event occurs or when the effects of differential power, resource problems or differing interests make it incumbent upon one party to raise the issue of concern to the other. Up until that time the party recognising the latent dispute will have been content to carry on with its work in the hope that either the potential dispute can be overcome or that circumstances will develop such that there is no need to pursue it further.

The dominant party is very often unaware of the existence of a latent dispute issue or of tensions between the parties, although the less dominant party may well have been aware of it for some time.

If no trigger event occurs, and if the less dominant party feels that overall it is not disadvantaged by the contract, then the latent dispute might never develop further. The less dominant party may be able, by the use of well-designed strategies, to overcome the latent dispute before it emerges into a full-blown dispute. This is the optimum situation and should be encouraged where possible.

Trigger events may result in expectations being revised or threats being perceived. These in turn change the status of longstanding but latent grievances, causing them to become a full-blown dispute. If these trigger events are recognised before they occur it should be possible to defuse potential dispute situations before they come into being. This must be the objective of all parties to a contract if they are to prevent escalation of the dispute and the inevitable costs that its resolution will entail.

1.2.2 Escalation/institutionalisation

As a dispute develops and extends over a period of time, so the chance of its escalation increases. Escalation is the increase in intensity of a dispute, often where substantive debate is overtaken by personal impressions, interests, distrust and confrontation. Escalation can change a tractable dispute into one that is virtually impossible for the parties to resolve without outside assistance.

There are five changes that occur when a dispute escalates.[2] These are discussed in greater depth later in this book, but the basic changes are:

- parties move from light tactics, such as persuasion, promises and compromise efforts, to heavy tactics such as threats and power play;

- the number of issues in dispute increases;

- issues move from specific to general, and relationships between the parties deteriorate;

- the parties to the dispute grow in number as other players get drawn in;

- the goals change from reaching a mutually acceptable compromise to winning at all costs.

Escalation can lead to the end of negotiations and the adoption of alternative means of resolving the dispute. There is a general worldwide trend, particularly noticeable within the UK and the US, to institutionalise these forms of ADR. This has the effect of taking the dispute out of the hands of the parties and placing it within the institutionalised mechanisms, to be resolved under the rules and procedures established by the particular institution concerned.[3] Such institutionalised provisions for dispute resolution have developed largely because of the reluctance of individual parties to opt for ADR voluntarily. Institutionalised ADR helps the parties overcome barriers which they would otherwise have been reluctant to cross, and contributes significantly to the settlement of disputes that have escalated beyond the inter-party negotiation stage. It is hoped that as this institutionalisation of ADR spreads throughout the EU, some degree of rationalisation of the laws, processes and procedures to be adopted will take place, so that there will be a uniform approach at least throughout all EU member states.

1.2.3 Negotiation

Negotiation of a dispute is the process of bargaining that takes place between the parties. At this stage discussions are held concerning the issues in dispute, aimed at achieving conciliatory give-and-take agreements that are mutually acceptable to each party.

The four primary stages in negotiations are:

- preliminary introduction of parties to negotiation;

- agreement on objectives of negotiation;

- negotiation process proper;

- review and finalisation of agreements reached.

Negotiation is as much about tactics as it is about being convinced of the strength of one's own case or about being totally familiar with all the commercial and technical aspects of the subject matter of the negotiations. It can be undertaken in an atmosphere of relative cooperation, as when all parties are seeking a solution that is mutually acceptable and beneficial (a win–win situation), or can be confrontational, where one or more parties intend to prevail over the others (win–lose situation).

The secret of successful negotiations lies in comprehensive and effective planning. Before the start of negotiations each party should consider the following points:

- Goals – what does it want to get out of the negotiations and what does it understand the other party wants?

- Trades – what does it have that it can trade and how comfortable would it be in trading it? Also what does the other party have to trade and would this trade be acceptable?

- Alternatives – what is its BATNA? Is this good or bad and how likely are the parties to proceed with this alternative?

- Relationships – what is the history of the relationship between the parties? Could this influence the negotiations, will there be any hidden agendas, and how can these be managed?

- Expected outcomes – what are the minimum acceptable results that each party would be likely to accept (bottom line)? What are the expectations of higher management and can these be accommodated or modified?

- Consequences – what are the consequences for each party of winning or losing?

- Power – who is the dominant party in the relationship? Who controls resources, including finances? Who stands to lose the most if agreement is not reached? What power does one party have to actually deliver the results the other party hopes to achieve from the negotiations?

- Possible compromise solutions – based on all the considerations, what possible compromises might be forthcoming from either party?

If the negotiations are only approached after first fully exploring these points, then each party should be more aware of its objectives, the methods it can employ in achieving them and the extent to which it can continue the negotiations before reaching the stage where it is clear that further negotiations would not be viable.

1.2.4 'Loop back'

There is little chance of negotiations being successful if one party believes that it will gain more by pursuing an alternative approach, such as using one of the recognised ADR procedures, than it would by continuing the negotiation. Very often, however, the alternative procedure does not run the full course and the parties agree to 'loop back' to negotiation. This would tend to happen after the parties have held several preliminary 'alternative approach' hearings and each has established the other's strengths and weaknesses to a greater extent than was possible during the original negotiations. The parties are then placed in a better position to work out a mutually acceptable negotiated settlement.

'Loop back' may not work the first time around, and it may take several attempts before a settlement can finally be reached. The advantage of taking the dispute out of the more formal procedure and back to the negotiating table is that by doing so the parties regain control of the settlement agreement, and so will not have one imposed upon them by the independent person or body authorised or empowered to do so under the ADR procedure.

1.2.5 Stalemate

Negotiations cannot always be successful and some will inevitably reach a stalemate situation. This need not automatically lead to a complete cessation of discussions and the instigation by one party of the next stage in dispute resolution required under the contract.

The first breakdown in negotiations, and maybe one or two subsequent breakdowns, can be classified as the 'hurting stalemate stage', where neither side can win but neither side wants to back down and accept a loss. Despite the parties' understanding that they have reached a stalemate in their negotiations they often find it difficult to transform their attitudes towards the dispute in the hope of reaching a settlement. Their views have become polarised and they are reluctant to compromise their opinions even though they are aware that this is probably the most sensible and cost-effective approach to take.

Leaders fear suffering a loss of face should they concede any of the points they have been propounding so strongly during the negotiations. They lose track of the most basic intention of the negotiations, which is to try to reach a settlement acceptable to all the parties to the dispute.

This is the optimum time for the parties to call a temporary cease to negotiations. They should withdraw and reconsider their attitudes towards the dispute, their tactics (both those which they have employed in the past and those which they need to consider using in the future), and the personnel who have been leading the negotiations to date. This is the time to decide upon the changes which have to be made to allow the negotiations to reconvene in a meaningful manner.

1.2.6 De-escalation

After the negotiations have been called to a halt following the acceptance by the parties that a stalemate situation has been reached, the parties should spend time reflecting on what they have achieved so far and what they should be doing to build on this to achieve a settlement.

The negotiating team that has represented a party up to this point may have gone as far as it can go and either the team itself or higher management might consider this to be the time for de-escalation measures to be introduced, possibly including changing some or all of the team members in order to bring new life to the negotiations. This need not necessarily mean a total change of the party's strategy, but should include a modification of its attitudes and objectives so that the other party gains a positive perception of its continuing intentions to negotiate to a settlement. Negotiations could then be resumed, with the new team offering the other party a chance of compromise which was not previously apparent.

If the reconvened negotiations fail, a decision has to be made on whether it is worth trying again or whether the time has come to call on the services of outside bodies to assist in resolving the dispute. The contract will in all probability contain specific requirements as to whether the dispute should immediately be referred to arbitration or whether there should be an intermediate stage adopting some other form of ADR, such as mediation or third-party adjudication.

Irrespective of what the next stage is, the parties should take time to prepare their cases with care and precision. It is hoped that this would have been done before the dispute negotiations started; however, it is far from unusual for parties to enter into a dispute negotiation scenario without adequate preparation. This is a deplorable situation and should be avoided at all costs. Even if such pre-preparation has been undertaken properly, each party should still take time to review its material, taking due consideration of both the impression it has gained of the other party's case and the supporting detail the other party put forward during the negotiation stage. The negotiations might have been held 'without prejudice', which would restrict the extent to which a party could introduce statements made and documents presented to the negotiation table in its subsequent representations.

1.2.7 ADR/arbitration

Various methods of ADR are available to the parties, and if the contract does not specify which method has to be invoked following a breakdown in negotiations, the parties are at liberty to agree on which method to adopt.

The ADR methods most frequently adopted in construction contract disputes are mediation and third-party adjudication. Arbitration, which is not generally viewed as an ADR method, is often a preferred option to litigation, albeit a potentially expensive one. It is not the intention of this book to explain in detail the application of these various methods of ADR as there are many books in the marketplace dedicated to this subject. It is worth mentioning, however, the benefits of adopting one of these should negotiations fail.

The most relevant benefits of these methods in the context of this book are:

- disputes are dealt with quickly and are controlled to a large extent by the parties;

- overall they are less costly than litigation;

- they encourage 'business' people to develop and adopt 'business' solutions to 'business' problems (i.e. the results are more likely to be based on commercial and business sense rather than on purely legalistic reasoning, although the latter cannot and must not be ignored in reaching the commercial decision);

- they allow for more creative remedies and outcomes compared with litigation;

- they provide a self-regulatory approach to dealing with disputes if managed effectively;

- they reduce the risk of bad publicity flowing from disputes and the concomitant lowering of morale;

- they offer greater confidentiality than does litigation;

- they reduce stress to all parties, with concomitant health benefits.

Whichever method is adopted, the parties must ensure that disclosure is full, clear and complete. Many disputes escalate due to misleading or incomplete information being disclosed or information not being fully understood by one party.

1.2.8 Settlement

Disputes are generally disagreements that involve negotiable interests. As explained above, the issues in dispute can generally be settled through negotiation, mediation, adjudication or arbitration. Disputes in the construction industry are generally relatively short term since they will relate to a project which has a defined contract period and they usually lend themselves to the development of mutually acceptable solutions. Dispute settlement is aimed at concluding the dispute and need not necessarily deal with its fundamental causes. However, unless the fundamental cause is eliminated a similar dispute could arise at some time in the future. Therefore, when reaching a settlement every effort should be made to ensure that the fundamental cause is identified and measures taken to eliminate it, or at the very least to prevent further disputes of a similar nature.

The final stage in a dispute will be settlement. This might be achieved by negotiation, in which case the parties should each be satisfied that they have achieved the best possible solution for them, or by ADR or arbitration, in which case one party might not be quite so content with the outcome. The main thing is that the dispute has been resolved and the parties can put the whole episode behind them and carry on with the execution of the project in which they are involved.

1.3 CAUSES

1.3.1 Organisational structure

The organisational structure of the parties' respective companies may have an influence upon how issues are dealt with, both within each organisation and externally. It may also influence how the companies are required to interface one with each other. The companies may have to incorporate a degree of flexibility into their operations to avoid disputes arising. This will enable the parties to develop systems that suit both their particular needs and the needs of the project in which they are involved, thereby increasing the likelihood of achieving its successful execution.

On a construction project there is inevitably a time when there is conflict between the site management and head office management. The greater the degree of interdependence, the greater the likelihood of communication difficulties and so the greater the scope for disputes to develop. This is frequently exacerbated by the rigidity of head office procedures, which have been prepared in isolation from and without due regard to the needs, limitations and priorities of site management. This can have a detrimental effect on relationships and on effective communication, not only between personnel within the organisation but also between the various organisations involved on the project, both at site and head office levels.

It is impossible to expect, and unrealistic to suggest, that all parties involved in a project should agree on the introduction of identical structures for each of their respective organisations. It is neither unreasonable nor unrealistic, however, to suggest that each party should ensure a degree of flexibility within its organisational structure sufficient for it to be able to interact with other parties' organisations such that the project teams are not hindered in any way by structural differences. There should not be any opportunity for interdepartmental disputes to arise purely because of organisational structures. Potentially contentious interdepartmental issues should have been foreseen and eliminated at the stage when the organisational structure was first introduced, or at least accounted for when such issues were recognised as posing or likely to pose a problem.

When establishing project- and site-specific organisational structures and procedures, due account must be taken of the particular structures of each party's organisation and of efforts made to ensure that these are accounted for, as far as is reasonable and practical, in the project organisation and procedures. This might require, for instance, something as simple as ensuring that a party's particular head office personnel are copied in on communications relating to a particular aspect of the project works. Similarly, where one party has required that all change decisions are referred to a head office director for sanction, the other parties adopt a similar approach, thus reducing the risk of disputes at a later date over the authority of a party's representatives on site to agree such issues on its behalf.

Excessive departmental interdependence can give rise to interdepartmental disputes, where one side of the interdepartmental relationship does not provide the other with adequate and timely information or performs inadequately in some other way. I have recently been involved in a large power plant rehabilitation project where significant delays occurred at the design stage. Our head office had taken on more projects than it was capable of handling at one time and the largest one was seriously in delay. All the company's design engineers were employed preparing documents to support both acceleration of the works on that project and the claim team's efforts in rebutting liability for delay. Due to the high level of liquidated damages on that project, the one I was involved in suffered design delays and eventually project completion delays. The result was that we too incurred liquidated damages, albeit of a lesser amount. Since these damages were in effect largely self-inflicted we had no option but to accept them. This situation could have been avoided if someone in head office had understood the implications of its actions and either employed extra in-house design engineers or given our project team the opportunity to engage external designers to assist us, the cost of which would have been considerably less than the liquidated damages we were obliged to pay the employer. Unfortunately, a rigid organisational structure prevented the head office team from permitting the project team to take this step.

1.3.2 Communication

As will be stressed in other sections of this book, great emphasis must be placed on establishing effective communication channels between the parties, and between the various team members representing those parties.

Even when communication channels have been established and agreed upon by all parties there is still a chance that communication within those channels will break down, or at least not be as effective as intended. The communication channels might even prove to be counterproductive if misapplied or misused.

Semantic difficulties can have a significant influence on the emergence of disputes, and if a communication is related to an activity that is critical to the performance of a task then a semantic misunderstanding can easily have catastrophic repercussions. This can occur in any situation, but it is a particular risk where the parties or their representatives are of different nationalities, or even from different regions of the same country, where their understandings of a particular word or phrase differ.

Any misunderstandings, not only those of a semantic nature, can lead to disputes. With this in mind all parties should ensure that communications between them are made in clear and concise terms and that any issues which could lead to contention are discussed openly, giving all parties the opportunity of raising points about which they are unclear or about which they have concerns. This gives the parties the opportunity to resolve all doubts and concerns at an early stage rather than leaving them to develop into disputes.

Where communication is document-driven it is wise to have procedures in place by which a document receipt is confirmed back to the issuer. In this way, misunderstandings over whether or not the document actually reached the recipient will be avoided. This is a simple process, whether the documents are delivered by hand or mailed in hard copy format or sent by email. Other means of communication may require more thought as to how receipts could be generated, possibly requiring that the more important documents, such as notices under the contract, be sent by recorded mail, registered mail or courier.

1.3.3 Contract

It is stressed in several places in this book that one of the most important measures that can be taken to avoid disputes is to understand the contract fully. Most of the contradictions and discrepancies should have been ironed out at the tender stage. Inevitably, however, not all such issues will have been either identified or resolved at that stage. The tender team was probably more concerned with winning a contract, and although they might have identified risks, contradictions or discrepancies, these might not have been followed through adequately in case the team's chances of success was prejudiced. The project execution team will look at the contract in a different way. They should also have access to the tender team's notes and discussions on proposed deviations, some of which may not have been incorporated into the contract documents.

Issues which are still unclear or which need further clarification must be brought to the other party's attention at the earliest opportunity and should not be left unresolved. Where a satisfactory explanation, modification or solution cannot be obtained by discussion between the project execution teams the issue should be referred to a higher level within a party's organisation. Alternatively, it may have to be referred to external third parties as required by the contract or by the procedural agreements reached by the parties at the outset of the contract. It should be possible to resolve potentially contentious contractual issues during the currency of the project works, hopefully soon after they have been identified as such, and to avoid their escalation into disputes.

1.3.4 Cultural and personal variables

Cultural and personal variables can cause disputes or influence their resolution. These variables can include the following:

- Conflicting needs – there may be conflict between a party's own needs and its contractual obligations. For example, there may be pressure from within the party's organisation for a particular project to be completed within a certain time period, perhaps due to financial constraints (e.g. to include profits within a particular financial accounting period). Alternatively, a party may have a particular political constraint (e.g. a local government authority requiring project completion before local elections in order to emphasise its contribution to the enhancement of the community amenities). A balance has to be found between satisfying the specific needs of one party while at the same time ensuring that the obligations and responsibilities of all parties under the contract are fulfilled. Once this balance has been established the parties should be able to work together to achieve an end result that satisfies all parties' respective needs. Architects and engineers have a particularly difficult role in such a situation. They have to balance their client's financial and technical needs with the various rules and regulations with which their design has to comply and with the contractor's ability and desire to perform.

- Conflicting styles – different organisations, and different groups and individuals within an organisation, have different styles of management and of applying themselves to interpersonal relationships. These sometimes clash with the styles and methods of those with whom they interrelate in the execution of the project works. Organisational styles are difficult to change. However, where one party's style is found to be in direct conflict with that adopted by the other party, careful consideration must be given to how the parties can establish the optimum working relationship. This might involve identifying team leaders within each organisation who have the flexibility, knowledge and experience necessary to understand the other party's style of working and who can introduce compromises to develop a style of management that satisfies the needs of both parties without compromising either's own organisational responsibilities. Where different people within an organisation have different styles of management, it might be that the style of a particular individual, if adopted on a particular project, would lead to poor working relationships, either within their own project team or with other parties. In such a case, higher level management should identify the issue and make appropriate changes, possibly replacing the particular team member on the front line with one whose style will gel better with those with whom they are obliged to interrelate, thereby reducing the risk of disputes. Different styles can include:

(i) compromising style, when equal strength opponents try and find a solution that will at least partially satisfy all parties, or when the cost of escalating the dispute is higher than the cost of losing some ground;

(ii) accommodating style, in which a non-assertive but cooperative party shows a willingness to meet the needs of other parties at the expense of its own needs;

(iii) avoiding style, in which the party takes a weak and ineffective approach and tries to evade the dispute entirely.

- Conflicting perceptions – different people can have different perceptions, at least to some extent, of just about everything that occurs. For example, if an accident happens on site, different people will have different perceptions of blame and responsibility. Similarly, if a new team member is appointed, different people will have different perceptions as to the reason for the appointment and of the benefits the new member's appointment is likely to bring to the project. The only way to prevent misconceptions is to be open and above board and to communicate fully at all times. In the first example above, an accident report should detail exactly what happened and why, with as much photographic, documentary and other factual and contemporaneous evidence as possible to back up the conclusions of the accident investigator. In the second example, a memo should be circulated to all concerned team members, including those of the opposite team, explaining the reason for the appointment, the role of the new appointee and the expectations as to what benefits will accrue from the appointment. In that way all team members will be looking at the situation from the same viewpoint and will 'buy into' the management perspective, thus limiting the chances of disputes arising.

- Conflicting goals – the project teams will have one overriding principal goal, which is achieving completion of the project, preferably within time and on budget. Intermediate goals, however, will differ and could give rise to conflict. We have all surely come across projects where the contractor's site manager's main goal is to complete within time, its commercial manager's goal is to complete within budget, and the project manager's goal is to complete at the very least within time and budget. The client and its architect/engineer will also want to complete within time and budget, but may have different ideas as to how this can be achieved. Unless the teams have one uniform goal, internal disputes will be inevitable. The site manager and the design, engineering and construction teams must all understand that time is not the only factor to be considered. The commercial manager may well take budget as the main focus, but will also be aware that time is money and so will be looking for ways to gain extensions of time where work is delayed and to ensure that all additional work is compensated for. The project manager must balance time and budget in order to achieve the best possible result, taking account of all the various influencing factors. The client and its architect/engineer must balance their own needs with an understanding of the problems the contractor has encountered, possibly resulting from instructions or variations issued by the architect during the currency of the contract. The project team must have one set of goals; these must be monitored regularly to ensure they are being met, and if not, to establish why not and to agree on the necessary measures to be taken in order to get them back on target.

- Conflicting pressures – effective communication and proper planning can eliminate the majority of conflicting pressures. As long as everyone knows what is happening, when and why, they should be able to identify areas of possible conflict in due time and discuss proposals for avoiding the potential conflicts. For example, in a factory refurbishment an overhead crane might be required on a particular week by the contractor to install new machinery at one end of the building and by the factory operator to unload stock at the other end of the building. By proper communication, these two events should be known to both parties well in advance of the time the events are due to start, and by proper planning the necessary changes could be accommodated. This could be achieved either by adjusting the programme to suit the alternative timing of one or other of the events, or an agreement could be made for the contractor and factory operator to use the crane at different times of the day, thereby maintaining the original programme. If there is no communication or proper planning, Monday will arrive and both parties will be in dispute over which event has priority and which party can use the crane.

- Conflicting roles – clear lines of demarcation must be drawn around team members to ensure that each is aware of their own role, responsibilities and duties. Where one team member is asked to perform a function that is outside their job requirements, or another member is asked to perform the same function, effectively duplicating their efforts, this can only be a recipe for disputes. Clearly defined and transparent management procedures will prevent such a situation occurring.

- Different personal values – different people have different personal values and this can be reflected in the way in which they approach their work. Management should instil in all staff that when they are dealing with company issues they should comply with company policy. If they have a problem with this then they should raise the matter to higher management, and either take part in a training session aimed at overcoming the problem or be transferred to another section where their own personal values would not be an issue.

- Uncertain policies – the absence of clear and concise company policies can create an atmosphere of uncertainty and conflict. It is strongly advised that one of the first documents prepared at the start of a project is a project management manual, which should be agreed between the client and the contractor. The manual should address the procedures to be adopted for all envisaged communications and interfaces between the parties, including all aspects of contract administration, from distribution of mail to recording minutes of meetings, application for change orders, submissions of notices etc. These issues might have been touched on in the contract documents, but these would probably have concentrated on the general obligations and responsibilities of the parties and would not have defined precise methods of document control, communication and interrelation. Where company policies change during the currency of the project it is important that all staff are kept fully informed and, where relevant, that other parties are also notified of the changes. If company policies are non-existent, it is even more important to define project policies in a project management manual. Otherwise, disputes between the various parties and within a party's own organisation will be an inevitable consequence.

1.3.5 Disputes in international arenas

The opportunities for contentious issues to develop into major disputes are far greater in international projects than is the case in homeland projects. This is largely because of the differing and sometimes contradictory cultural, religious and traditional influences which are encountered on a day-to-day basis in an international environment.

It is important on international projects for the project team to include local staff who are familiar with, and who can inform the expatriate team members of, local customs, traditions and general business methods that must be followed if their work is to be carried out effectively. Local staff members should explain the cultural and religious traditions that must be followed and should explain what would happen if they were rejected. I recall working on a power plant project in South East Asia with a contractor who initially refused to adopt the national tradition of asking the local Buddhist monk to bless each milestone achieved on the project. When the first generator was installed the project manager declined the local staff's pleadings and carried on without arranging for the traditional blessing. The following night the generator exploded into flames, setting the whole project back six months. No cause was ever found, but the project manager insisted on each subsequent milestone event being blessed and no further problems were encountered.

In addition to religious, cultural and traditional influences, international contracts have to contend with the added, and possibly more obvious, issue of compliance with local laws, rules, regulations, ordinances, standards etc. These will hopefully have been researched at tender stage, in which case there should be a complete package of relevant documents ready for handover to the project execution team.

In the absence of such a handover package the project team should make the assembly of such a package one of its primary objectives. Now that so much information is available over the internet, this is not such a daunting task. There are many websites that provide English language translations of relevant documents, many of which do not even expect a subscription or payment of any kind. The translations may not be 100 per cent accurate though, and it is advised that, if you find a contentious issue, or its solution, in a downloaded document, you should have the translation checked by a translator licensed by relevant officials in the country concerned.

1.3.6 Justice – inequalities of power and influence

A major cause of many disputes is the search for justice. A party may feel that it has been unfairly treated and will embark on a course of action to remedy the perceived injustice. This situation must be recognised for what it is at an early stage and action taken to defuse it otherwise it will lead to a dispute.

The perceived injustice might be real or imaginary, but it will, nevertheless, be a very real threat to the progress of the project unless it is addressed. The aggrieved party will not readily change its perception unless the other party, which it views as having more power and influence on the contract than it has, takes some measures to redress the perceived imbalance. The most effective way of showing that there is no inequality is to establish a joint working group comprising members from each party and to give that working group the power to decide issues which an aggrieved party is concerned about. In this way it would have an equal voice, and the other party would have the opportunity to explain the reasoning behind its original (contentious) stance in a calmer and more evenly balanced environment.

The way in which some forms of contract are written, in particular the currently applicable FIDIC family of contracts, increases the likelihood of a contractor believing that the client has more power than it does, as the contracts are evidently weighted in the client's favour. It is normal for the party lower down the commercial tree to feel that the party above it has more power, based on the principle that the higher party holds the purse strings and hence must have more power. If the contract is well thought out and is applied correctly this need not be to the detriment of the party lower down the tree. Unfortunately, those in this position tend to feel inequality from the time they first become involved at the tender stage. They seldom exert as much influence as they should over the content of the contract they intend entering into for fear that, should they confront the client in any way, they might lose the opportunity of tendering, not only the current contract but also for any subsequent projects.

CHAPTER 1 SUMMARY

1. Dispute avoidance is in reality nothing more than a blend of good commercial management and project management.

2. Dispute management must be based upon a well thought out strategy; it does not merely 'happen'.

3. Communication is a critical and decisive element in the process of dispute avoidance. It depends on the parties' desire to prevent a dispute arising, their willingness to communicate and an environment in which such communication can take place.

4. The core concepts applicable to dispute situations are:

    i.   the conceptions the opposing parties have of each other and the attitude with which they approach the dispute;

    ii. the grievances the parties hold against each other;

    iii. the goals each party sets to change the effect and nature of their grievance;

    iv. the means each party uses to achieve its goals, including in particular the level of communication skills employed in the avoidance or resolution of a dispute.

5. In a win–lose situation, one party is prepared to win at all costs and does not particularly care about the other party's interests.

6. In a win–win solution, the parties both feel positive about the negotiations and each considers that they can benefit from them in some way.

7. A lose–lose situation occurs when one party becomes obsessed with making the other party lose at all costs and common sense and reason are ignored.

8. It is likely that parties contemplating a long-term relationship would only settle for a win–win solution; anything less would undermine their long-term intentions.

9. Escalation is the increase in intensity of a dispute, often where substantive debate is overtaken by personal impressions, interests, distrust and confrontation.

10. Escalation can change a tractable dispute into one that is virtually impossible for the parties to resolve without outside assistance.

continued. . .

11. Negotiation is as much about tactics as it is about being convinced of the strength of one's own case or about being totally familiar with all the commercial and technical aspects of the subject matter of the negotiations.

12. The secret of successful negotiation lies in comprehensive and effective planning.

13. Establish effective communication channels between the parties and between the various team members representing those parties, including their architects, engineers and other consultants engaged as part of the management team.

14. Understand the contract. The process of understanding starts with the tender team and continues with the project execution team, both of which must fully understand the contract's requirements and implications.

15. Cultural and personal variables can cause, or influence the resolution of, disputes.

16. A perceived injustice might be real or imaginary, but it will, nevertheless, be a very real threat to the progress of the project.

Notes

1. Rubin, JZ, DG Pruitt, and SH Kim, *Social Conflict – Escalation, Stalemate and Settlement*, McGraw-Hill, New York, 1994, p.252.

2. Theory propounded by DG Pruitt and JZ Rubin.

3. 'Courts will encourage the use of ADR at case-management conferences and pre-trial reviews, and will take into account whether parties have unreasonably refused to try ADR or behaved unreasonably in the course of ADR' – The Rt. Hon. Lord Woolf MR in the Final Report on the Civil Justice System in England and Wales [1996 LCD], Chapter 5.

The nature of disputes

2

2.1 INEVITABLE DISPUTES

2.1.1 Clash of cultures

A clash of cultures used to be experienced primarily when working on overseas contracts, but it is increasingly becoming a factor in domestic projects. It may be a little extreme to refer to a 'clash' of cultures, but unfortunately a clash is what often occurs.

'Culture' is defined as 'the customs, ideas, values, etc of a particular civilisation, society or social group, especially at a particular time'; culture therefore does not relate solely to nationality.[1] In fact there are often quite significant cultural differences between people from different parts of the UK and these have to be considered when establishing the contract team.

I recall once discussing a short-term consultancy with the project manager of a large and well-known international company based in Manchester. When the time came to discuss terms and logistics the project manager asked me where I was living. I said 'Swansea' (South Wales), to which he replied 'we might just as well employ someone from Pakistan'. That was in the 1980s when such remarks were offensive but not uncommon: today, such a comment would probably fall foul of one of the myriad new laws, rules and regulations. This small example serves to illustrate a potential clash of cultures within a UK environment. Needless to say, I did not take up the consultancy we were discussing, and I doubt the employer took on anyone who was not English. If I had represented the other party to the contract there would without doubt have been 'inevitable' disputes based purely on the culturally biased attitude of this company's project manager.

Such experiences are not uncommon, and many a team has been disrupted by similarly biased cultural attitudes. It is impossible, undesirable and unrealistic to attempt to build a team of people all of whom come from a similar cultural background, and even more so to build a team that matches the cultural background of the other party to the contract. It is possible, however, to build a team composed of people who do not have concerns about cultural differences. It can even be a positive benefit to have a culturally diverse team, as this can bring new perspectives to the management of the contract.

2.1.2 Clash of personalities

Personalities vary irrespective of the cultural backgrounds of the people concerned. Some people are more aggressive than others, some concentrate on the 'big picture' whereas others are only concerned with what happens in their sphere of operation, some enjoy interaction with their colleagues and opposite numbers whereas others tend to be 'loners'. People who come from different educational backgrounds may have different ways of approaching their work; those who have been trained 'on the job' possibly having a more practical approach than those who have trained by attending full-time university courses.

2.1.3 Clash of personal, professional and business ethics

It is highly likely that personal or professional ethics will clash with business ethics at some time in everybody's career. When this occurs a judgment has to be made on which set of ethics should be allowed to dominate the issue. There are good ethics and bad ethics, ethics being defined as 'rules or codes of conduct'. Those rules or codes of conduct may have been set by a professional institution, company management or in the simplest form by parents. Some may be generally perceived as better than others, and some may fit in with a person's own moral standards better than others.

Where your professional institution has established a code of ethics that you must comply with in your business life then there is no alternative to abiding by it. Failure to do so will result in some form of disciplinary action being taken by your institution, the severity of which will depend upon the particular code of ethics that has been broken. If your company policy requires a different or lower ethical standard to be adopted than set by your professional institution then you have two options: either refuse to abide by the company policy or resign. If your company policy requires a different but not necessarily lower ethical standard than your own, then the decision is a personal one and will depend upon how significantly the company policy offends you.

The other party may have different ethical standards to those which you, your professional institution or your company subscribe to. This could result in a clash unless you are able to maintain your ethical approach without compromise. If the other party's ethics offend you or have an adverse effect on your performance, this is a potential dispute situation and has to be addressed. If your approach to the execution of the project can remain constant despite the clash of ethics with the other party then the decision that needs to be made will be whether the effect the other party's ethics has on you can or cannot be accepted. The only two options to be considered if a dispute is to be avoided are to accept that there is a difference in approach that will have to be lived with or to reach a compromise that satisfies you both.

2.2 INTRA-COMPANY DISPUTES

In addition to avoiding disputes with other parties it is equally important to avoid disputes within your own company. Such disputes can be disruptive within the company, within the project teams and for the other parties involved in the project. Intra-company disputes can arise for a variety of reasons but for the purposes of this book we will concentrate on those which are procedural in nature, those which are management related and those which are progress related. Avoiding disputes in these areas will allow the project to run smoothly.

2.2.1 Procedural

The project team could be composed of long-standing company employees or it could be a mix of old and new employees and/or consultants engaged for the specific project. However the team is made up, its members have to gel together for the team to be effective, although this is not always an easy process. Personnel who have worked for some time under the direction of one manager within the company might not appreciate the approach taken by another manager in the same company. Although they might both be abiding by the same company procedures, they might deal with them in different ways. Alternatively, the company might not have invested in an established set of procedures, in which case this deficiency needs to be addressed. Other personnel might have joined the company from another with a different way of working, and may be finding it difficult to accept the change.

Procedures need to be consistent in every case, but they also need to be sufficiently flexible to allow different teams to adapt them to suit different projects.

As soon as a potential conflict situation is noticed senior management responsible for the execution of the project should intervene and direct the team members as to which procedures should be followed. They should explain why this is the case and identify the benefits to the company of adopting them. This is the point where anyone who is not happy with the procedures should raise their concerns and initiate a dialogue, from which the team members should emerge in agreement on how to proceed. The dissenting member may be able to persuade the others that their way is best. The most important thing is to have consistency within the project team and to eliminate the chances of a dispute arising over these issues.

2.2.2 Management related

Management can, if it is not careful, lose sight of the difficulties involved in executing a project within budget and on time. It would be surprising if they were not concerned about both these elements, but management's role is to see the bigger picture and sometimes 'political' issues can take precedence. The one project with which you are concerned might not feature as significantly in the big picture as you would wish or imagine.

For example, management has decided, based on knowledge not available or relevant to the project team, that the party with whom the company are involved on the current project may be worth cultivating with a view to future, more significant work. As a result, it may be considered acceptable to take a loss on the current project in the interests of that future relationship.

Such an issue can, if not handled sensitively, result in a dispute between the project team and management. Management needs to explain to the team the benefits of adopting a specific approach to the project, even though the team might not fully agree with it (such as carrying out extra work or accelerating the works without seeking reimbursement). The perceived benefits might include continuity of work for the company, or even a bonus for the team if future work is secured as a result of the success of the initial project.

Management may also have to answer to a board of directors and shareholders. They will need confidence not only that current work is being executed correctly and in the company's best interests, but also that management is looking forward and taking whatever steps are necessary to maintain full order books for the coming years. This is a balancing act which management must be able to control while ensuring that staff are aware of the reasons for and buy into the strategies adopted. This is one of the principal attributes of good management.

2.2.3 Progress related

Different departments within an organisation have different views on progress and its place in the 'big picture'. It goes without saying that progress is important if the works are to be completed within the period defined in the contract. However, commercial considerations are also important.

Disputes can arise when those responsible for the physical execution of the works clash with those responsible for ensuring the commercial viability of the project. Architects/engineers and quantity surveyors often encounter such a clash and have to sit back, appreciate each other's concerns and find a workable solution. Site managers are usually more concerned with 'getting the job done on time' than ensuring, as the commercial managers expect, that it comes in 'within budget' or that the company is recompensed for any additions or changes to the work.

Such disputes can be avoided by including the project execution team in the commercial discussions at an early stage in the project. Time taken explaining the role that the site team can and should play in ensuring the commercial viability of the project will prove to be time well spent. Even then, the project execution team's natural inclination will be to put time considerations above cost considerations. Measures should be taken to keep the project on a commercial track, such as the introduction of standard reporting systems and pro formas to be completed when specific situations arise, such as delays on site, requests for additional work etc. If delaying events can be identified at an early stage then extensions of time can be agreed as the project proceeds, giving the project execution team a new target date for completion without the fear of incurring liquidated damages, and hopefully with the additional costs incurred being reimbursed by the client.

2.3 INTER-COMPANY DISPUTES

2.3.1 Contract interpretation

A significant percentage of disputes experienced on contracts based on non-standard forms of contract are related to the interpretation of contract clauses. This seldom occurs when one of the standard forms is used as their clauses have been tried and tested over a period of time and most companies using them are aware of their interpretation or are able to obtain guidance on their use. Standard forms have also been well tested in the courts, and reference to relevant case histories will often clear up any confusion.

If you are not dealing with a standard form of contract, or if you are dealing with one of the many hybrid forms (adapted from standard forms by employers to suit their particular needs), you will need to make yourself familiar with the clauses and how they are to be interpreted. This must be done at the very start of your involvement in the project. If you do what the contract requires then you should not face any major contractual problems. However, to be able to do this you need to understand the clauses, how they interrelate, and how the contract's drafter intended them to be applied.

Ideally, this familiarisation should be undertaken as part of the risk assessment exercise carried out by the tender team prior to submission of the tender bid. However, this is not always the case. As soon as the contract is awarded and the project execution team is established, the team should, if one has not already been prepared, undertake its own risk assessment of the contract. Any clauses that are unclear should be brought to the attention of the employer and clarification should be sought. This is the first point in time when contentious issues arising from a contract clause are likely to arise, and if these are not resolved then the chances of a later dispute arising are increased. It is important to continue the risk assessment exercise throughout the life of the project and it should be made a priority task on all projects. Unfortunately, the period immediately following the contract award is a time when everyone is working frantically to get the project off the ground and so risk assessment is often overlooked.

Similar situations occur with consortium agreements and joint venture agreements. These agreements should as far as possible mirror the terms and conditions of the main contract, where applicable, in order to ensure that the parties to such agreements share the same rights, obligations and responsibilities on a back-to-back basis. The terms and conditions should again be agreed before the tender is submitted, but frequently they are not given adequate attention until just before work commences. By that time the consortium or joint venture partners will have committed themselves to the project, and invariably the more powerful partner dominates in the negotiation of the agreement between them. The less dominant partner tends to fear that if it disputes any of the terms and conditions included in the agreements at tender stage it might prejudice its chances of involvement in the project. It fails to recognise that it might have been better off financially had it held out rather than accepting terms and conditions that can only lead to disputes and potential losses during the project execution stage.

2.3.2 Time – progress/sequence of works

A common cause of disputes is the programming of works, which affects a party's ability to achieve the completion date set down in the contract. If the project has been set up and managed as it should have been there will be agreed contract programmes and also regular updates to track progress. Proper programme control is a management tool that all parties can benefit from. However, this is not an ideal world and unfortunately programming is often neglected in order to devote more time and resources to actually getting the project going.

Often it is only when it is clear that the anticipated contract completion date is not going to be achieved that all parties start thinking about programmes. The employer will ask for a revised programme showing how the contractor intends to pull back lost time or showing a new completion date. The contractor will be looking to programme analysts for support of its claim for an extension of time. Unless there was an agreed contract programme, and unless there have been regular updates, neither party's requirements are likely to be satisfied.

In order to reprogramme the works to take account of all delays experienced there must be a baseline programme that can be adjusted. This might have been submitted to the employer for information purposes or for approval, or prepared by the contractor for its own internal use. The employer may only recognise a programme that it has approved, or at least received for information purposes. It is unlikely to give any credence to one prepared by the contractor for its own internal use, unless it was included in its tender package. It is possible, however, that a contractor's internal programme could be introduced in evidence at a later date should it need to justify a claim.

In summary, to avoid a dispute concerning time it is essential for a programme of works to be agreed between the parties at the earliest opportunity. If the contract does not require a programme to be agreed then it will probably require one to be submitted for information at a specific stage or stages in the works. Whatever the contract asks for must be complied with: this is likely to include regular updating of the programme and the submission of further updates when the contractor can see that its work is falling behind. This fits in with the two basic tenets of dispute avoidance: communication and contemporaneous records.

2.3.3 Cost – payment, extras, omissions etc.

Probably the most common causes of disputes are those relating to money. These will include contractors' requests for recovery of additional costs incurred because of delays for which it considers itself free of liability, and costs incurred because of changes to the works requested by the employer. Employers' cost claims will include requests for savings resulting from omissions or negative adjustments of work, application of liquidated damages provisions, drawdowns on bonds and warranty issues. The contract will usually contain procedures in respect of all such issues and these should be followed at all times.

Subject to any particular clauses in the contract, if the employer instructs the contractor to change, omit or carry out additional work then the contractor should immediately confirm this in writing to the employer, and should not execute the changes until the employer has confirmed its instructions in writing. Ideally, the contractor should in its initial response to the employer give a quotation covering the cost and time impacts of the instruction, and the employer, in its confirmation, should either accept the estimates or commence negotiations on them. If this is not done in a timely manner and the cost negotiations are carried out at a later date then contemporaneous records of what work was actually done, by whom and when, will play a significant part in the contractor's justification or the employer's rejection of the additional costs claimed.

Similarly with liquidated damages and bond drawdowns, if the contractor has records which show clearly that it was not responsible for the issues that the employer contends made deduction of liquidated damages or the drawdown on bonds an available option, then it will be able to use those records in its defence should the dispute escalate.

2.3.4 Quality – specification, standards, fitness for purpose etc.

Standards of workmanship and materials will be specified in the contract documents. The documents will also specify how quality is to be controlled and the level of proof that the employer will expect from the contractor to show that it is complying with these requirements. If the contract is silent on these points then the scope for disputes arising increases considerably.

The contract may require the contractor to submit a quality control/quality assurance procedures manual in the very early stages of the contract. This document will explain how the contractor intends to control quality, both at site and at the premises of major subcontractors and suppliers. It will state when and where tests will be carried out and will give the employer the opportunity of witnessing those tests as appropriate. It will define the documentation to be provided, such as test results, quality records, inspection sheets, welding records, as-built drawings etc.

Disputes can and do arise when the product fails to match expectations. The employer may blame the contractor for lack of supervision, use of inferior materials, lack of control of subcontractors and suppliers or similar, and it will be up to the contractor to prove otherwise. Again, communication and contemporaneous records will be of paramount importance. It might well be that the employer is correct and the materials are not up to standard, in which case the contractor will have to revert to its subcontractor or supplier for recompense.

The best way to prevent disputes arising is to comply with the requirements of the contract and follow the quality control/quality assurance manual to the letter. Alongside this the contractor should maintain all possible contemporaneous records so it can show at a later date that such compliance did in fact take place. These same records will also identify where the true responsibility lies for an observed defect and so enable the contractor to pursue the offenders from a position of strength.

2.4 INTRACTABLE DISPUTES

2.4.1 Destructive nature of dispute

An intractable dispute is a dispute that seems to stubbornly elude resolution no matter what techniques are employed by the parties. Sometimes referred to as a destructive dispute because of the way in which the adversaries approach it, it is a dispute that has a low probability of being resolved. It is very often a dispute that is personality- or emotion-driven rather than one based on more tangible issues. For instance, if an employer and contractor disagree on how much should be paid for a particular item of work, the dispute is based on a tangible issue and can be resolved by negotiating a mutually acceptable sum. However, if the employer and contractor disagree simply because of a clash of personalities fuelled by the fact that they do not like each other, the dispute is driven by emotions, and it is unlikely that a simple solution will be attainable.

An issue-based dispute can easily develop into an emotion-based dispute, and this must be avoided at all costs. Pursuing a destructive dispute will inevitably make matters worse. It is often better to leave it unresolved and to focus attention on reducing the intensity of surrounding issues in the hope that this will contribute to a reduction in the intensity of the destructive dispute. If the nature of the dispute is such that no actual damage is being caused whilst it remains unresolved, and if the parties are basically unaffected by its existence, then the dispute cannot really be classified as intractable and it is probably best ignored.

Dispute avoidance is more pertinent to destructive disputes than constructive disputes: the latter can usually be resolved by discussion and negotiation but the former cannot. Dispute avoidance is not so much about preventing issue-based disagreements as reducing the amount of conflict generated by behaviour, emotions and ways of communicating, which create unnecessary and unresolvable disputes. Issue-based disagreements will always arise in a construction project situation whatever measures are taken to eliminate them. The secret is to establish procedures which ensure that they are minimised, and that those that do occur are dealt with effectively at the earliest opportunity and are not left to develop into destructive/ intractable disputes.

2.4.2 Impossible to resolve within a short timeframe

An intractable dispute will frequently be one that starts as a low-key contentious issue primarily apparent in the mind of only one of the parties, and which festers over a period before developing into a full-blown dispute. By the time the issue is apparent to all the parties it is often too late to take steps to reach an amicable resolution. An intractable dispute will inevitably persist over a long time and will often hinder progress on other areas of the project works, either directly through the particular issues concerned or indirectly by having an adverse effect on the relationship of the parties to the dispute.

2.4.3 Resists all attempts to resolve

By its very nature an intractable dispute is one which does not lend itself to an early solution, and all attempts to resolve it are stonewalled by the emotion/personality-based attitudes of the parties concerned. The very fact that efforts are made to resolve a dispute and that these efforts fail to bring about a conclusion contributes to the dispute being classified as intractable. It may well be that the goals set by one party for resolution of the dispute are viewed by the other party as particularly damaging to its objectives and costly in terms of time, money or both, and do not appear to lend themselves to compromise. The dominant party may feel that it can resolve the dispute only by the use of force, be it commercial or contractual. That approach will inevitably contribute to an acceleration of the dispute's destructiveness and intractability.

2.4.4 Fundamental disagreements

Intractable disputes usually arise from disagreement on fundamental issues. They are not necessarily related to particular technical or commercial issues, but are based more on emotions and differences in personalities, ultimate goals or aspirations to dominate. Disputes which involve irreducible high stakes or win–lose issues that have no apparent area of possible agreement often become intractable. Because of the fundamental nature of such disputes there is little likelihood of reaching a solution as long as the parties see no way out; one or both parties must give up on an objective which is paramount to their perceived view of success.

2.4.5 Pursuing and resolving an intractable dispute

As mentioned above, there is always a fear with a destructive/intractable dispute that pursuing it will only make matters worse, unless the personalities responsible for the initiation of the dispute are kept well away from the resolution process. It is a fact that the attitudes that brought the dispute into being will, unless curtailed, contribute to its escalation. The way in which words are spoken and opinions given, even the body language and phrasing used by the parties, is the main obstacle to resolution of an emotion- or personality-based intractable dispute.

Conflicts can arise simply because of the manner of communication: the words chosen and the tone employed. To this end it is imperative that steps are taken to ensure that all communication is in a civil manner and respects the other parties' entitlements to their own opinions, irrespective of the fact that these may not always be agreed with.

Intractability is not a real characteristic of a dispute but is merely a perception held by the parties to the dispute. Perception is an important influence of action and so cannot be ignored. Resolution of the dispute is reliant largely on changing the perception of the intransigent parties to the dispute. It is each party's duty to explain its opinion clearly and concisely using facts which the other party can relate to and understand in the context of the dispute, and which will encourage it to change its perceptions both of the dispute and of the likelihood of the parties being able to reach a mutually acceptable settlement.

It is no use denying that an intractable dispute exists, rather both parties should make every effort to put a positive spin on it and transform the dispute from a destructive one to a constructive one. This might not result in a full and final solution being found, but may well result in a partial solution being agreed and the identification of a 'way forward' in respect of those aspects still in dispute. The reduction in the extent of the dispute should go a long way to reducing its overall classification from 'intractable' to 'tractable'.

2.5 HEALTHY DISPUTES

2.5.1 Constructive disputes

Not all disputes have a detrimental effect on the relationships between and within the parties to the dispute: on the contrary, many bring long-lasting benefits. Disputes can serve to highlight deficiencies in the way that a company operates, in the way that it trains its employees and in the attitude with which it approaches projects in general and areas of potential dispute in particular.

As a result of experiencing a dispute situation, management may be encouraged to set up specialist training courses for staff to help them identify potential areas of dispute and to show them how to deal with the negotiation process. The very exercise of opposing parties sitting down together and resolving a dispute between them can, if managed properly, bring the parties closer together and give them a sense of bonding, which can only bring benefits to their future working relationships.

2.5.2 Conflict should not be feared

The worst approach to an impending dispute is to be afraid of it. Fear can encourage a party to accept a solution to the dispute that it is basically unhappy with, and this in turn results in resentment by the aggrieved party. This resentment can affect the parties' relationships on the current project and can also carry on into other projects that they are, or intend to be, involved in, making life more difficult for them both.

Approach each dispute without fear and put forward the best case you can offer in support of your opinion. If you do not have a strong case yet you still wish to pursue the dispute then this may be the only time when a certain amount of trepidation may be justified. If your case is weak then the issue concerned should not have reached the stage where it becomes a fully fledged dispute: it should already have been settled amicably.

2.5.3 Conflict can result in growth

Dispute negotiations, if controlled and handled confidently, and with both parties behaving and responding in a realistic, concerned, respectful manner, can give each party confidence in its ability to handle a dispute situation. This applies whether a party won or lost. In either case if the person responsible for the negotiations felt that they had performed well then he or she will be better prepared to act the next time a similar situation arises.

At a company level, a company called into dispute negotiations by a larger company might consider its chances of success limited purely because of its size. If it ends up

winning then it will grow in confidence and will approach future negotiations in the knowledge that it cannot be browbeaten by larger rivals and that its team is equal to anyone's.

2.5.4 Conflict can result in innovation

When faced with a dispute each party will review and analyse the facts of the case before taking further steps. If a compromise is considered a possibility, the parties should consider how that compromise might be effected. This could result in innovative solutions being put forward which in the end benefit the project. Had the issue not escalated to dispute level then such a solution might never have been considered. The solutions introduced to resolve the dispute may well produce innovations that can be introduced into the next project from the very beginning, thus bringing benefits to that and subsequent projects that would not have been available had the dispute not arisen.

2.5.5 Conflict can result in new ways of thinking

In a similar vein, the parties to a dispute will probably have been debating the issues concerned for some time before the escalation into a full-blown dispute. The very fact that the parties have now to sit down at the negotiating table with each other will focus their minds on examining how the issues in question were allowed to escalate into a dispute. From this examination the parties will discover any shortfalls in the performances of individuals within their organisations, and they will have the opportunity of rectifying those shortfalls, not only in respect of the particular project concerned but also in respect of future projects of a similar nature. If the issues being discussed had not been allowed to escalate into a dispute, the parties might never have discovered those shortfalls and would by inference not have benefited from the improvements subsequently introduced.

2.6 UNHEALTHY DISPUTES

2.6.1 Emotion-/personality-based disputes

Some disputes are healthy and bring about change that benefits all concerned. However, there are also unhealthy disputes that do no one any good. Disputes that are based on emotion, personality traits, lies and injustice are all examples of unhealthy disputes. These can be avoided in part by establishing good personal relationships, by eliminating personality conflicts through careful selection of team members, and by establishing clear lines of communication between the parties and between the members of each party's team.

When contentions are based on facts there is a good chance of resolving them before they reach the dispute phase, but where they are based on emotions, clashes of personalities or lies, or are caused by feelings of anger, regret, vengeance, self-esteem or self-image, the chances of reaching a solution are more remote since these feelings cannot easily be dispelled by facts.

2.6.2 Benefit from continuation of dispute – profiteering

In some situations potential disputants are aware that they can in fact benefit by continuation of the dispute. I am currently involved in a situation involving a main contractor and two subcontractors whose work is falling behind schedule. If the work of one of the subcontractors is not completed within the next six months, it knows that the existing plant it is modernising will have to shut down and cease operation because a significant part of this subcontractor's rehabilitation work is necessary to ensure that the plant complies with EU regulations coming into force at that time.

The employer has proposed rescheduling the work in such a way that all past delays are forgotten about, and liquidated damages which would otherwise have been due are waived, as long as all parties will agree to the new schedule for the remaining work. The main contractor and one subcontractor are happy to accept the employer's proposals and are prepared to reschedule their work as per the employer's request, as are all the local sub-subcontractors.

The remaining subcontractor, whose work is essential for the plant's continued operation after the EU rules come into force, refuses to agree to the employer's proposal. It is well aware of the criticality of its work and knows that the longer it holds out the more desperate the employer will become to agree to its terms in order to keep the plant in production. To shut the plant down would prove extremely expensive to the employer and, in this particular situation, to the country in which it is situated.

The subcontractor intends to hold out until it is offered sufficient financial incentive to accelerate its work in the possibly erroneous belief that the longer it continues in dispute the greater the benefits it will gain.

This is a dangerous game to play since the employer could insist to the main contractor that the dissenting subcontractor is removed from the project and replaced by a more cooperative one. The danger in this to the employer is that delays to project completion and some period of total plant shutdown might not be avoided, but the time comes when practical considerations are overshadowed by ones dictated by internal, and in this case national, politics.

Profiteers of this kind are difficult to protect against as no amount of cooperation, communication and relationship building will deter them from their strategic goals.

The only way to prevent this type of situation happening is to make sure that there is strict schedule control in place from the outset, and that situations such as that described above are noticed and dealt with before they get to the point where profiteers are able to use them to their own advantage.

CHAPTER 2 SUMMARY

1. Avoid disputes within your own company as these can be disruptive within the company and the project teams and for the other parties involved.

2. Company procedures need to be consistent but sufficiently flexible to allow different teams to adapt them to suit different projects.

3. Management has to see the wider picture, and your project might not feature as significantly in this picture as you would wish or imagine.

4. Do what the contract requires and you should not face any major contractual problems. However, to be able to do this you need to understand the clauses, how they interrelate and how the contract drafter intended them to be applied.

5. To avoid a dispute concerning time it is essential that a programme for the works is agreed between the parties at the earliest opportunity.

6. Proper programme control acts as a management tool which all parties to the contract can benefit from.

7. If the employer or its architect/engineer instructs the contractor to change, omit or carry out additional work, then the contractor should immediately confirm this in writing to the employer and should not proceed in the execution of such changes until they have been confirmed in writing.

8. Each party should maintain all possible contemporaneous records so that they can be used at a later date to support, justify or defend against claims.

9. Dispute avoidance is more pertinent to destructive disputes than constructive disputes; whereas the latter can usually be resolved by discussion and negotiation, the former cannot.

10. Dispute avoidance is not so much about preventing issue-based disagreements as reducing the amount of conflict generated by behaviour, emotions and ways of communicating, which create unnecessary and unresolvable disputes.

continued. . .

11. An intractable dispute does not lend itself to an early solution and all attempts to resolve it are stonewalled by the emotion-/personality-based attitudes of the parties concerned.

12. Intractability is not a real characteristic of a dispute but is merely a perception held by the parties to the dispute.

13. Perception is an important influence of action and so cannot be ignored.

14. Do not deny that an intractable dispute exists, but put a positive spin on it and transform it from a destructive one to a constructive one.

15. Many disputes bring lasting benefits. Innovations and management changes introduced to resolve a dispute may produce solutions that can be introduced into the next project, bringing benefits to that and subsequent projects that would not have been available had the dispute not arisen.

16. The worst approach to an impending dispute is to be afraid of it.

17. If a person responsible for negotiations feels that they have done their best and presented themself well, then they will be better prepared to act in a similar situation in future.

Note

1. *Chambers 21st Century Dictionary*, 2nd Edn., Chambers Harrap, 2000.

Potential sources of dispute

3.1 CONTRACT CONDITIONS

3.1.1 Interpretation of clauses

Many construction-related disputes have their roots in misinterpretation of one or more clauses in the contract. The misinterpretation may go back as far as the tender stage, when those responsible for preparing the tender did not fully understand the meaning of a particular clause and the repercussions only become apparent after the contract had been signed and work was underway.

It is important that the tender document is analysed before the tender is completed and that a risk assessment is carried out on a clause-by-clause basis. In this way the true meaning and impact of each clause will be understood and will have been addressed before the contract is signed. This applies particularly to the contractual and commercial clauses, but it has equal relevance to the technical specification clauses, many of which could have contractual or commercial relevance if misinterpreted. The review format shown in Figure 2 illustrates one of the ways in which this exercise can be carried out. This example is designed for use in a review of proposed deviations. As negotiations progress, and the deviations are allowed or rejected, the analysis could include values representing the likelihood of the remaining risks occurring during the currency of the contract, using scores of 1 for a low risk to 10 for a high risk.

Where the clause is unclear it should not be ignored, nor should 'best guesses' at its meaning be attempted based on past experience or unproven assumptions. It is a simple process to ask the employer for clarification and explanation, and its response will usually be circulated to all those contractors participating in the tender process so that each will be tendering on exactly the same basis.

The risk assessment sheet, any interpretations and/or explanations provided by the employer, and any actions implemented or agreed upon as a result of this exercise should be passed on to the project implementation team so that they are aware of what has been agreed and what is expected of them. This minimises the number of disputes likely to occur during the course of the contract through misinterpretations of this nature.

Where a clause that was not given any particular attention in the pre-tender risk assessment becomes significant during the project execution stage because of confusion as to its true meaning, then a similar review will be necessary. This can be carried out by the party raising the issue. However, if the results show that the clause might lead to a contentious issue, then it would be sensible to involve the other affected parties in the interpretation process. This would allow a consensus of opinion to be reached before any action is commenced.

Fig. 2 Risk Analysis

Bid/Contract Title: .... **Date:**.................

Clause No. (Note 1)	Analysis of Risk (Note 2)	Level of Risk: Exposure (Note 3)	Level of Risk: Consequences (Note 4)	Evaluation of Risk: Comparison against Criteria (Note 5)	Evaluation of Risk: Set Risk Priorities (Note 6)	Identify Options (Note 7)	Evaluate Options (Note 8)	Set Strategy (Note 9)

Notes:
1. Insert document section/volume number and clause number of relevant clauses
2. Include relevant extract from clause and define the perceived risk
3. Evaluate from the other information available the likelihood of exposure
4. Describe the possible consequences of exposure
5. Compare what the effects of the risk would be against, for instance, the proposed programme for the works, works of other contractors/owners etc.
6. What are our priorities, is the risk 'acceptable' in terms of the overall project strategy, how acceptable is it in relation to other aspects of the bid/contract?
7. What are the options available? E.g. propose deviations to bid or add clause to clarify position, accept risk, insure against risk, pass risk on to subcontractor etc.
8. What would be the effects of each option in terms of cost, time and political impact (relationship with client, future work etc.)?
9. Propose most effective strategy, taking into consideration all aspects of risk analysis as identified

3.1.2 Application of laws, ordinances, regulations, by-laws etc.

Tender and contract documentation will include references to the application of particular laws, ordinances, regulations, rules, by-laws etc. Many will be internationally recognised, but many will relate to the particular project or employer, or to the country in which the contract has been signed or in which the project is to be executed.

Each reference must be scrutinised in much the same way as described for the interpretation of contract clauses. Even laws, standards, codes etc. that you might consider yourself to be familiar with need to be reviewed to ensure that there have been no revisions or updates since the last time you used or reviewed them.

When dealing in a foreign country, particular attention needs to be given to local laws, rules, regulations etc. Many will have been written in the language native to that country and the copies available for review may well be translations. Unless the translations are official translations prepared by the body responsible for issuing the original documents, or are issued by a translation service approved by them, they will need to be checked and verified independently as having the same meaning as the original documents. Disputes frequently arise through reliance on translations which, when checked against the originals, have mistranslated a critical word or failed to give due emphasis to a particular requirement. A relatively small expenditure at the outset can save a considerable amount of time and money at a later date.

3.2 TECHNICAL SPECIFICATIONS

3.2.1 Interpretation of clauses

The technical specifications will have been reviewed in detail when the tender price was prepared. It is likely that they will have been given more attention than some of the conditions of contract, as their close scrutiny will have been necessary in order to obtain quotations for and to price the various elements of the work involved.

Misunderstandings may still occur, particularly if the technical specification review was carried out by technical specialists, who might not recognise the contractual or commercial implications of the matters being reviewed. One of the worst scenarios would be that the specialist did not realise that they had misinterpreted an item, or had chosen to ignore the issue, and had designed or installed an item in line with their own company's practices. When it was discovered that their interpretation of the employer's needs was incorrect the redesign or replacement of the incorrect item would present a major problem, with all the delays and extra costs that would be associated with such work.

To understand the employer's requirements fully, time should be spent cross-checking the obligations and responsibilities that the technical specification imposes upon the parties with those that the conditions of contract impose. It is not unusual for these two sets of documents to have been written by different consultants working for the same employer, or even by two departments within its organisation, and sometimes coordination between the two breaks down. In such a case it will be necessary to refer back to the contract agreement to establish which documents have precedence and to establish the true extent of the obligations and responsibilities expected of each party.

3.2.2 Application of standards, rules, regulations etc.

The technical specifications will include references to various standards, rules, codes of conduct, company regulations etc. that have to be adhered to during the execution of the project works. These will impose constraints on the designs and the methods of installation and construction to be adopted. If you are used to dealing with a certain set of standards, say the German DIN standards, do not assume that other standards mentioned in the technical specifications will be similar, even if they are widely accepted and highly reputable international standards. Company rules and regulations might also include restraints on access to site, restrictions on working hours, labour agreements etc.

All specifications need to be thoroughly checked to ensure that the proposed design and construction method conform to the specific requirements of the contract. If equipment delivered to site is inspected and the employer discovers that it has not been manufactured to the specified standard, the cost of replacing it will be felt not only in money terms but also in the additional time taken to procure, manufacture and deliver the item in compliance with the technical specification, risking delay to completion of the project.

3.3 DRAWING AND DOCUMENT REVIEW

3.3.1 Approvals

It is usual to find a clause in a contract which spells out in some detail the procedures to be followed as regards the review of drawings and documents, such as schedules, quality control plans, health and safety plans, erection procedures etc. These must be followed to the letter in order to avoid disputes.

Care must be taken to understand fully which drawings and documents have to be submitted for approval by the employer and which are to be submitted for information purposes only. If there is any doubt, check with the employer or its consultant at the earliest opportunity. Any delay caused by misinterpretation of the employer's requirements could well be held to be the contractor's responsibility, depending upon the actual wording of the relevant contract clauses. If a document has been submitted in the belief that it was for information purposes only and fabrication or construction has been commenced based upon that drawing, when in fact the document submission actually required the employer's approval, then it would be a major setback if the employer subsequently raised this issue and declined approval for a justifiable reason.

The contractor should be required to maintain a drawing register, such as that suggested in Figure 3. The register should contain details of all drawings submitted, the dates of submission, dates of return, whether approved, rejected or returned

Fig. 3 Drawing Submission Record Sheet

ID No.	Drawing No.	Title of Drawing	Purpose of Submission*	Rev No.	Submittal No.	Submission Date	Return Date	Return No.	Remarks	Status **
001	sk/b/9000/01	Roof plan	A	00	E/B/103	21/07/07	12/10/07	C/B/57	54 days late	3
002	sk/e/7601.07	Electrical layout	A	03	E/E/139	22/07/07	19/09/07	C/E/39	on time	2
003	sk/b/9467	Paint schedule	I	06	E/D/76	24/10/07	20/11/07	C/D/10	on time	n/a (I)
004	sk/b/9708	External works	A	00	E/EW/54	27/10/07	12/12/07	C/EW/17	18 days late	5
005	sk/b/9976	Workshop plumbing	A	08	E/P/167	30/10/07	19/12/07	C/P/28	23 days late	4
006	sk/b/0083	Car park layout	A	00	E/CP/26	30/10/07	17/11/07	C/CP/22	on time	2

*   A – for approval; I – for information
** 1. Pending   2. Approved   3. Approved with comments   4. Under revision   5. Rejected

with comments and any delays beyond the period for approval stipulated in the contract. This register should be submitted to the employer each month with the monthly report. If any questions arise at a later date as to why a particular section of work was delayed, a quick check of this register will immediately show whether this was in fact due to late submission or late approval of any specific drawing.

Where approval is required the contract should be specific as to the period within which such approval, or rejection with reasons, should be given by the employer. The same clause should specify that failure on the part of the employer to approve or comment within the specified time would give the submitting party the right to consider the drawing or document approved (deemed approval) upon the expiry of such period. Deemed approval, if claimed, should be confirmed to the employer as soon as the approval period has expired in order to avoid a later dispute.

3.3.2 Reviews, comments and amendments

Where drawings or documents are submitted for approval the employer will have the opportunity to reject them completely or to request amendments; in either case it should clearly state its reasons. In the latter case the employer should detail the exact amendments required and state a period, if not provided for within the contract, within such amendments are required.

An alternative would be for the employer to approve the drawings subject to certain comments. In fact, the comments might not require amendments to the submission, but could relate to such matters as the timing of the works concerned (e.g. work to start only after the occurrence of another related event, or to take place at night).

The status of returned drawings should be recorded in the drawing register. The register should identify which were approved, which were rejected, which were approved with comments, which are still pending and which are being revised by the contractor.

If amendments are required the submitting party must ensure that it complies exactly with the requirements listed in the instructions accompanying the returned documents or as otherwise issued. Once the amended drawings or documents have been submitted it is usual for the same review periods to be allowed as were allowed for the initial submissions, and also for the same provisions to be made for further comment by the employer. At that stage, however, any further comments or requests for amendments would be limited to comments on, or requests for amendments to, the amended drawings based upon the initial comments made on the original or immediately previous submission of the drawings/documents. If the employer requires new amendments that were not previously requested, and which would not seem necessary taking into account the initial brief, initial submission and initial comments, then this request could well be taken as a change in requirements, warranting the issue of a change order. This should be raised immediately so that the parties have the opportunity to resolve the issue before a dispute develops.

3.4 PROJECT MANAGEMENT

3.4.1 Progress management, control and amendments

One of the main areas where disputes can arise is in relation to progress. As mentioned earlier, it is usual to submit a programme at the beginning of the project (which may or may not have been subject to the employer's approval) and to monitor progress against it on a regular basis. In the course of monitoring progress it should be possible to detect when certain items of work are falling behind schedule. These issues should be looked into immediately with a view to searching out the causes. The earlier the causes can be identified the earlier corrective action can be taken and the better the chance of avoiding a subsequent dispute arising.

Where the causes are internal, within your own company, the action should be reasonably easy to implement as long as there is the will within the company to do so. If the employer is found to be responsible in some way for events leading to the delay in execution of the works the employer should be informed immediately, and meetings convened to discuss methods of overcoming the delays for which it is considered responsible.

Once the delay cause has been identified and the responsible parties have discussed the problem and decided on methods of overcoming it, action should be taken to resolve the issue. This might involve amendments to drawings, documents or methods of working and, if agreed to be necessary, the contract time or price may need to be adjusted as appropriate.

Project controls are the most cost-effective way of avoiding disputes by identifying situations that might, if not dealt with promptly, escalate into disputes. Project control systems cannot solve all problems on their own; the issues the controls throw up must be dealt with promptly and effectively and this can only be done by human interaction. If the vital elements of human cooperation are not in place then all the controls in the world will not help a project.

3.4.2 Site management issues

Site management, as opposed to project management, refers to the management of the technical and physical processes used in the execution of the works. This is obviously a minefield when considering the opportunities for misunderstandings and disputes, and so it is of critical importance that each and every issue that could end up as a dispute is handled, promptly and efficiently, and in a way that defuses any dispute before it arises.

Site management has a tendency to prioritise completion on schedule, and can lack commercial or contractual awareness. Of course this is not always the case, but is a tendency found more in site management teams than project or commercial management teams.

Site managers, whether working for the contractor, the employer or the employer's architect or engineer, must have it instilled in them from the outset of the project that great importance is placed on good communication, both between the parties and within each party's project team, and on early attention to issues that are or could become contentious. The commercial members of the team need to be made aware of any construction or technical issues that could affect the commercial viability of the project, or that could become a cause for dispute with the other party. These might not always be easily identified by someone who is not continually monitoring the actual construction works, and so close cooperation within the project team is essential.

Site management has two principal facets, one involving the contractor and one involving the employer and/or its architect/engineer. The different parties might not always have the same view on particular methods of executing the works, and the contract will probably give the contractor the opportunity to use methods with which it is more comfortable and experienced rather than dictating precise methods of execution for each particular item of work. For this reason it is wise for the contractor to submit method statements to the employer in respect of major items of work well in advance of the work being carried out. This will ensure that any other party's views can be addressed and overcome at the earliest opportunity. Otherwise, work already started may have to be stopped because the employer has reason to be opposed to the particular method chosen, based perhaps on previous bad experiences, misconceived conceptions or clashes with other ongoing works on the same site.

3.5 COMMERCIAL MANAGEMENT

3.5.1 Cost control – payment issues

All parties to a contract will be interested in managing cost control in respect of their individual budgets. However, the ways in which the parties manage their affairs will not necessarily coincide, and this could, if not properly coordinated, result in disputes.

The contract will define payment terms between the employer and the contractor, and similar agreements will be in place between the contractor and its subcontractors/suppliers. These will usually state that payment will be made within a specified number of days from the date of issue or receipt of an invoice. From this it could be assumed that disputes should not arise as far as payment periods are concerned. This is by no means a certainty.

One area of potential dispute could be the invoice itself. The contract may be specific as to when an invoice can be issued, for example when a certain specified milestone has been reached or achieved. Unless there is a clear definition of what has to be completed in order for the parties to be able to confirm that the milestone has in fact been reached or achieved, this issue is itself open for dispute. I have worked on projects where milestones have appeared to have been reached, only to find that the contract includes references to additional tasks that have to be completed before the actual milestone certificate of achievement can be issued, such as fire safety precautions being completed, spare parts having been delivered etc. These additional issues are often overlooked and result in invoices being rejected.

Other issues that can lead to rejection of invoices include disagreement over measurements, where the invoice is based on measured quantities of work having been executed during the invoice period, shipments claimed as delivered being found to be missing ancillary components whereas the payment terms require full delivery, and goods delivered or installations carried out being claimed by the employer to be defective or otherwise not in accordance with the contract requirements. All of these can be avoided if the project is managed effectively and efficiently with close coordination, communication and cooperation between the parties, joint inspections, joint measurements and prior agreement on exactly what has to be carried out before a payment can be requested.

The contractor will want to be paid as soon as possible for work carried out in order to maintain its cash flow. The employer on the other hand will prefer to delay making payments for as long as contractually possible, perhaps to maximise the interest it can earn on cash in the bank, to minimise ithe costs of borrowing money to finance the project works, or so that payments it has to make occur subsequent to its receipt of its own income. Prior agreement on payment terms and on a payment schedule will minimise the chance of disputes arising, as will close cooperation and communication between each party's management teams.

3.5.2 Variations to contract work – omissions and additions

No project will be built exactly as described in or required by the contract documents. It is inevitable that some changes will be made. Changes may be initiated by the contractor or the employer and could be proposed for a variety of reasons, including increased efficiency of the facilities being constructed, reduction in the time needed for completion of the facilities, introduction of improved materials, equipment or construction techniques etc. The employer will desire the most up-to-date facility at the cheapest possible cost and would prefer that any changes necessary to ensure this are carried out at no extra cost. The contractor's desire on the other hand will be to complete the project within the time and cost constraints imposed upon it by the contract, and it will expect recognition in terms of extra time and money in respect of any changes required by the employer. If the contractor proposes changes, the employer is unlikely to agree to increase the contract price or the period for completion of the works unless there is some tangible benefit to it that outweighs such considerations.

From this it can be seen that there is ample scope for disputes to arise unless the whole issue of change is handled with care and diplomacy. If the employer issues an instruction requesting a change then it must confirm any verbal instruction in writing, and the contractor must have the opportunity of submitting its proposal and reaching agreement on the cost and time effects of the instruction before work commences. The contract will probably include rules to this effect that need to be followed strictly. It might also make provision for any instructions that are necessary on health or safety grounds to be carried out immediately and for the associated time/cost effects to be agreed later.

Disputes should not arise if the contract requirements regarding changes are followed. However, disputes will arise where the change itself is disputed. The employer might consider its instruction to be merely a confirmation of something that it believes the contract already requires the contractor to carry out. The contractor, however, might consider it to be a change or addition to the contract. Where the facts surrounding the need for an instruction are not clear, discussions need to be held to determine where the responsibility for such work lies before it is implemented.

If the instruction results in work being omitted from the contractor's scope of work, the contractor may well have grounds for claiming additional payments. This could occur, for instance, where certain work has already been carried out abortively in connection with the omitted work or where the contractor has already authorised the commencement of work on the design and/or manufacture of specialist equipment, materials or similar. Such a claim could also relate to loss of profit on the omitted work. These issues need to be taken into account when the instruction is first considered and the relative merits of implementing the instruction or for declining to do so must be evaluated before proceeding further.

3.6 QUALITY ASSURANCE AND QUALITY CONTROL

3.6.1 Quality assurance

Quality assurance (QA) can be defined as the process of checking or reviewing work tasks, processes and/or services to ensure they conform to the employer's requirements or other specified levels of quality. In order to minimise the potential for disputes over partiality, QA is usually conducted by personnel independent of the mainstream project management unit responsible for the task or process.

QA includes the development of project requirements that meet the needs of all relevant project members and external agencies, planning the processes needed to achieve the required quality standards, providing equipment and personnel capable of performing tasks related to project quality, documenting the quality control efforts and, most importantly, performing checks to verify that the product meets the standards specified in the contract. If these checks are properly executed the incidents of disputes relating to quality of the product provided will be considerably reduced.

3.6.2 Quality control

Quality control (QC) is the measuring, testing and/or inspection of a task or process, and the checking of designs and calculations to ensure compliance with the requirements of the contract and of any standards with which the contract works have to comply.

3.6.3 Quality assurance/quality control plan

The principal tool used in maintaining quality assurance is the quality assurance/ quality control (QA/QC) plan. The contract usually requires a plan to be issued within a matter of weeks of the signing of the contract. This ensures that all parties are aware at an early date of the standards of quality control to be expected, the stages at which quality inspections and tests will be applied, and the resources necessary to ensure that the plan can be implemented, monitored and controlled. The plan should identify which quality standards are relevant to the particular project and determine how they are to be satisfied.

The QA/QC plan will include the following quality elements, each of which, if applied as proposed, will help to reduce the possibility of a dispute arising at a later date:

- Management responsibility – describing the quality responsibilities of the management stakeholders.

- Documented quality management system – explaining the standard quality procedures currently being implemented within the organisation.

- Design control – specifying the procedures for design review, design approval, design changes and non-enforcement of specific design control requirements.

- Document control – defining the process to control project documents at each project phase.

- Purchasing – quality control and quality requirements for subcontracting.

- Inspection tests – detailing plans for compliance and acceptance testing.

- Non-conformance – defining procedures to handle any type of non-conformance work, including defining responsibilities, conditions and availability of required documentation to make the non-conformance process work (e.g. the use of non-conformance reports (NCRs) each time a non-conformance is discovered, identifying the non-conformance and the remedy required).

- Corrective actions – describing the procedures for taking corrective actions in respect of problems encountered during execution of the project works.

- Quality records – describing the procedures for maintaining quality records (test and inspection reports, executed checklists etc.) during project execution and thereafter as necessary.

- Quality audits – internal audits to ensure the quality assurance team is performing in accordance with its brief and with company expectations. Audits should be scheduled on the basis of the status and importance of the activities to be audited and should be carried out by personnel independent of those having direct responsibility for the activity being audited.

- Training – specifying any training that the project execution team might benefit from in fulfilling their roles from a quality assurance point of view. Appropriate records of any training carried out should be maintained as part of the project documentation.

If the quality plan is comprehensive and if members of the project execution team are trained in the plan's aims and objectives and the methods expected of them in implementing it, then the main opportunities for disputes should be eliminated or at least significantly reduced.

3.6.4 Tests and inspections

The QA/QC plan will specify what tests and inspections are to be carried out during the course of the project execution. If items of material or equipment are being manufactured or assembled off site it is usual for the contractor to inspect the quality of the work from time to time. Depending upon the nature of the work and the requirements of the contract it is likely that the employer will be given the opportunity of attending such inspections with the contractor. The employer may attend the inspection, or may appoint a consultant to attend on its behalf. If the employer declines the offer to attend the inspection the contractor should provide it with a written report soon after the inspection has been completed in order to minimise the chance of a later dispute. The report should contain photographs, documents, updated manufacturing schedules and whatever else is required under the contract to satisfy the parties that work is progressing satisfactorily.

A similar sequence should be adopted in respect of tests. These may be required under the contract or by the standards to which the manufacturers are working, and again the employer should be given the opportunity of witnessing any tests along with the contractor. Test results should be documented and circulated to all parties. Where the results show that a test was failed, work should be initiated to bring the items up to standard and further tests should be carried out until the requirements of such standards are met.

If there is a later dispute as to the quality or efficiency of the items subjected to inspections and tests under the QA/QC plan then the records of any inspections or tests will serve as valuable evidence in the contractor's defence.

3.6.5 Approval

It is more than likely that the contract will make provision for the period allowed for consideration and approval of the QA/QC plan by the employer in much the same way as it will in respect of approval of drawings, as discussed earlier. Similar measures should be taken to ensure that the correct documents have been submitted. If the employer makes any comments on them or requires changes to be made, these must be actioned and the documents resubmitted for approval as soon as possible. It is doubtful whether the employer would allow work to commence until the QA/QC plan had been approved, but this would depend upon the precise wording of the contract. Once the QA/QC plan has been approved there should be no room for dispute regarding the intentions set out in the plan: the only disputes that could occur would relate to the method of implementation of the plan and to any issues thrown up during such implementation, such as unsatisfactory inspection results or failure of tests.

3.6.6 Documentation

Documents produced by and for the project are as much in need of quality control as are any other elements of the project work. As part of the QA/QC exercise, procedures should be prepared to control the preparation and submission of all documents and data that relate to this element of the project works. This will include such items as method statements, reports, calculations, standards and record drawings. Procedures shall identify and control the generation, distribution and confidentiality of such documents and data, and introduce a system to identify, collect, index, file, maintain and dispose of all such records and data, whether in hard copy or electronic format.

All documentation and data should be properly reviewed and approved for adequacy by authorised personnel prior to issue. A master document list should be maintained identifying the current revision status of each document or item of data at any given time. This will not only help to ensure that only the latest revision is being worked on at any time, but will also help clear up contentious issues regarding when a particular revision was issued or when an approved document was available, thereby eliminating a particular source of potential dispute.

3.7 HEALTH AND SAFETY AWARENESS AND CONTROL

3.7.1 Implementation of laws, site rules and regulations etc.

Health and safety issues are becoming more and more important in all aspects of life, and in no area can this be seen more than construction. Legislation in recent years has imposed increased demands on companies to adopt a proactive approach to health and safety, including preparation of detailed health and safety risk assessments and health and safety plans, and the provision of adequate health and safety training for all persons working on a construction project. Health and safety risk assessment is a legislative requirement in the UK placed on all employers and the self-employed.

The tender team will have taken due account of all relevant national and local health and safety related laws, rules and regulations when preparing the bid. The team should also have considered the particular health and safety rules and regulations imposed by the employer on its own staff and on outside companies working within its premises. If these have not been considered then there will be potential for disputes when compliance becomes an issue. Any compliance issues should come to light at the early stages of the project, when the contractor will in all probability be expected to submit its health and safety plan to the employer for approval.

The Health and Safety at Work Act 1974 in the UK defines the parties' obligations in reasonably clear and understandable English. It introduces the concept of 'so far as is reasonably practicable' and a quantum scale of risk which advocates that the management of risk is a balance between the risk and the time, trouble and cost needed to manage it. If this approach is adopted as recommended it should help to keep the management of health and safety issues in proportion and prevent the imposition of unnecessary safety measures. If health and safety is managed in accordance with the flexibility introduced by the Act then the chance of disputes arising should be reduced. A similar approach should be used in whatever country the project works are being executed.

3.7.2 Adequate staff training

Health and safety training is essential for ensuring legal compliance and should be provided to all staff. This should have as its principal aims and objectives:

- appreciation of health and safety law;

- appreciation of the legal duties of employers and employees;

- an overview of corporate responsibilities for contractors, subcontractors, agency personnel, visitors etc.;

- understanding of the different types of law that impact on health and safety, including common, civil and criminal law;

- understanding of the penalties available for breaching relevant laws;

- understanding of the language and methodology of the risk assessment process;

- an introduction to the practical application of relevant health and safety laws, rules and regulations by way of risk assessment matrices, check sheets etc.

By the end of the training all staff members should have a basic understanding of health and safety as it affects them in the execution of their particular roles in the project execution team. They should also have a broad understanding of how it affects the other members of their team and the other parties, sufficient to enable them to interact effectively with each other concerning health and safety issues. In this way disputes over health and safety issues should be minimised.

3.7.3 Accident control, recording and reporting

Accidents are a major cause of dispute since by their very nature they are not planned events and responses are of necessity reactive. It is essential that systems are put in place to both prevent and deal with accidents. The likelihood of accidents occurring will be greatly reduced if adequate health and safety measures are implemented and adequate health and safety training undertaken at the early stages of the contract. The potential for dispute will inevitably increase once an accident occurs and responsibility has to be allocated, so any measures taken to mitigate its effects will contribute to the chances of reaching an early settlement on issues of responsibility.

As soon as the accident occurs those responsible for health and safety matters must ensure that full and complete records are maintained of the causes for, circumstances surrounding and effects of the accident. These records will become increasingly important as the parties attempt to allocate responsibility. They will also be necessary for the design and implementation of measures to ensure that such an accident is not repeated. Without proper and full contemporaneous records different people will naturally have different recollections of the events. These recollections might be similar, but they might vary considerably depending upon the attention that the respective witnesses paid to the events, their preconceptions about the circumstances surrounding the accident, the period of time that has elapsed between the accident occurring and the witnesses being questioned, and any interests that they have in the settlement, including which party their loyalties lie with. Just because they are employed by one of the parties does not necessarily mean that their loyalties to that party will encourage them to try and 'cover up' the actual events, but it might well influence their judgment. Contemporaneous records, in particular witness statements and electronically dated photographs taken at the scene, should be compiled into a report which should be issued to all parties to the contract. This will help the parties sort out the facts from the impressions and will make a significant contribution to preventing dispute escalation.

3.8 INSURANCE CLAIMS

3.8.1 Establishing full extent of claim and claim responsibility

When events occur which could become the subject of an insurance claim, all parties must quickly take whatever steps are necessary and possible to establish the full extent of the claim and to allocate responsibility.

The lengths to which a party would need to go to establish the full extent of a claim will depend upon the exact terms and conditions of the contract and of the insurance policy under which any such claims would be made. In any case it would be necessary to establish cause and effect. Cause might be relatively simple to identify, but establishing the effect could be a more difficult task and would again depend to some extent upon the limitations of liability defined in the terms and conditions of the contract and in the insurance policy documents. In order to prevent disputes arising in respect of limits of liability it is important that the terms and conditions are thoroughly researched, understood and amended as necessary during the tender or contract negotiation stages. If any aspects of liability are in any way vague, contradictory or open to interpretation, and if these are not clarified between the parties before the contract is signed, it is likely that disputes will arise. The most onerous liabilities that can arise in such cases are those relating to consequential damages and loss of profit, and it is usual for these to be specifically defined in the contract as 'excluded' items. Liability is usually capped, sometimes at the contract price, but again this depends upon the wording of the actual contract.

The full extent of damage caused by the claim event will include not only the pieces of equipment, materials or sections of work that need to be repaired or replaced, but also any delays that the insurance claim works bring about and the costs associated with those delays. The most effective way of minimising disputes regarding extent and responsibility is for the contractor, the employer and the insurer (or its loss adjuster) to meet and jointly review all the facts. This will ensure uniformity of approach and a sharing of results, thus obviating the chances of disputes arising in these respects.

3.8.2 Maintaining adequate records

As soon as an insurance claim event occurs efforts must commence to ensure that full and complete contemporaneous records are maintained. The records should cover not only the event itself, but also the measures taken to establish the cause, effect and responsibility and to implement remedial works. The intention is that these records will show that each party has acted promptly and effectively within its own remit to establish cause and responsibility based upon the information available to it, and to implement remedial works in a proper manner. These will prove invaluable at a later date should one of the parties or the insurer (or its loss adjuster) assert otherwise. Failure to maintain such records will leave the door wide open for one of the parties to claim that inadequate efforts were made either to establish cause and effect or to mitigate the extent of remedial works necessary.

3.8.3 Loss adjuster

Insurers will in most cases employ a loss adjuster to investigate a claim on its behalf. It is worth noting that the loss adjuster's role is to save the insurance company money and is probably being paid on results, i.e. the more the loss adjuster reduces the value of the claim the greater their fees from the insurance company.

In addition to possessing a thorough knowledge of insurance and of the area in which they work, loss adjusters advise both the insurance company concerned and the policyholder on repair and replacement techniques. The contractor may be of the opinion that it is better to replace all damaged works, whereas the loss adjuster might consider it cheaper and no less effective simply to replace the damaged parts, and after discussions with the policyholder will advise the insurance company accordingly.

The loss adjuster will visit the policyholder within days of submission of the claim form to discuss the circumstances of the claim. The loss adjuster will check that:

- the loss or damage falls within the terms of the insurance policy;
- the sums insured on the policy are adequate;
- the amounts being claimed are fair and reasonable;
- all valid items of claim have been included and nothing omitted.

Loss adjusters can often point to aspects of the claim that the policyholder may have overlooked. They can also advise on repair techniques and will know of specialist firms in the area who can undertake work in connection with the claim.

The loss adjuster reports their findings and recommendations to the insurance company. The company is then in possession of the full facts on the matter and is able to make a decision based on the loss adjuster's findings and recommendations.

Disputes will arise if the loss adjuster's decision is not acceptable to the parties. For example, the contractor might prefer to replace a damaged unit with a new one in order that its function in relation to other units incorporated in the works can be relied upon and that contractual warranty provisions are maintained. This would probably also be preferred by the employer, and so the two parties may decide to lobby the insurance company requesting that the recommendations of the loss adjuster are not followed in their entirety. The final decision lies with the insurance company, but the more facts that the parties can put forward to justify their opinion the greater their chance of success. If the insurance company listens to their concerns and rejects all or part of the loss adjuster's recommendations then cooperation between the parties will have paid off and a more serious dispute will have been avoided.

CHAPTER 3 SUMMARY

1. The tender document must be analysed before the tender is completed and a risk assessment carried out on a clause-by-clause basis.

2. Cross-check the obligations and responsibilities that the technical specification imposes upon the parties with those that the conditions of contract impose.

3. Understand which drawings/documents have to be submitted to the employer for approval and which are to be submitted for information purposes only.

4. Project controls are the most cost-effective way of avoiding disputes. They allow identification of situations that might, if not dealt with promptly, escalate into disputes.

5. Project control systems cannot solve problems on their own. The issues the controls throw up must be dealt with promptly and effectively and this can only be done by human interaction.

6. If the vital elements of human cooperation are not in place then all the controls in the world will not help a project.

7. Site managers, whether working for the contractor, the employer or the employer's architect or engineer, must understand the importance placed on communication – both between the parties and between the individual members within each party's project team – and on early attention to issues that are or could become contentious.

8. Most payment disputes can be avoided if the project is managed effectively and efficiently. There must be close coordination, communication and cooperation between the parties, joint inspections, joint measurements and prior agreement on exactly what has to be carried out before a payment can be requested.

9. Disputes should not arise in respect of changes if the contract's requirements are followed. Problems will and do arise, however, where the change itself is disputed.

continued. . .

10. If quality assurance checks are properly executed then the incidence of disputes relating to quality of the product provided will be considerably reduced.

11. The principal tool used in maintaining quality assurance is the quality assurance/quality control (QA/QC) plan.

12. Test results should be documented and circulated to all parties. They will be valuable evidence if there is a later dispute as to the quality or efficiency of the items subjected to inspections and tests under the QA/QC plan.

13. A master document list should be maintained identifying the current revision status of each document or data sheet at any given time.

14. The management of risk is a balance between the risk and the time, trouble and cost needed to manage it.

15. The most effective way of minimising disputes regarding the extent and responsibility for accidents is for the contractor, the employer (or its architect or engineer) and the insurer (or its loss adjuster) to meet and jointly review all the facts, thus ensuring uniformity of approach and a sharing of results.

16. Contemporaneous records must be maintained regarding not only the accident event itself, but also the measures taken thereafter to establish the cause, effect and responsibility and to implement remedial works.

Dispute avoidance techniques

4

4.1 KNOW YOUR CLIENT/PARTNER

4.1.1 Due diligence

At the bid enquiry stage your company will have carried out a due diligence investigation of the party inviting the bids or the party with whom you are considering entering into a joint venture or partnership agreement for the execution of a particular project. This will be a comprehensive investigation based primarily on a commercial and legal appraisal of the status of the company concerned. If the bid is successful this information should be passed on to the project team for information purposes.

Once the bid has been made and the contract signed it can be assumed that the initial due diligence investigation must have provided satisfactory results. It could well have identified a number of issues which warranted mention in the risk assessment, and these will be evident from the risk register.

The project team will have other concerns and will need to carry out due diligence investigations of its own at a different, more practical working level. These investigations will cover the employer, employer's consultants, partners and intended subcontractors and suppliers. The project team will be keen to know all it can about how the other parties behave in a similar contractual situation and how they are likely to react in a team situation.

The due diligence investigation will consider everything from the other parties' understanding of contracts, and the obligations and responsibilities they impose upon them, to background information on the personnel appointed by the other parties to execute this particular project. Discussions with local subcontractors and suppliers who have had previous dealings with the employer concerned will throw light on its approach to payments, ethical behaviour, treatment of staff, relationships with relevant authorities etc., all of which will have a significant bearing on the successful completion of the current project.

The more background knowledge that can be obtained at the outset the greater the scope will be for dispute avoidance. The well used phrase 'know your enemy' has never been more pertinent, where the word 'enemy' in this context refers to 'employer' or 'partner'.

4.1.2 Previous involvement

The construction industry works in and alongside a number of different 'communities', including the energy sector, the gas/oil exploration sector, the commercial sector, the industrial sector, the residential sector and the leisure sector.

Each of these sectors is a close community and so it is likely that workers and management will have worked with or for several of the various players within each community at various times in their career.

Employees of a large company may be able to locate someone within their company who has previous experience of the employer, consultants, partners or subcontractors concerned. Approaches should be made to that person to explore all aspects of the other party's business outlook and ethics. First-hand information of this nature is invaluable, but it has to be used in the knowledge that it might have been influenced to some extent by personal relationships, feelings and emotions. In addition the company will have records of any disputes that arose when it was last involved with this other party, and these should be able to identify why these disputes arose and how they were dealt with.

Any previous knowledge held by your company that might assist your project team in understanding the other parties should be passed on at the earliest opportunity. This exercise should be ongoing throughout the course of the project, as and when new members join another party's team or new subcontractors and suppliers are appointed.

4.1.3 Create cooperative relationships

The importance of creating and maintaining cooperative relationships with all other parties involved in the particular construction project concerned is stressed throughout this book. The information gained from the various due diligence exercises can be used to build bridges and encourage cooperation between the parties. If the other party's particular strengths and weaknesses are known it is possible to work in a way that will build mutual trust and cooperation. It is not necessary to emphasise the other party's weaknesses, as that will only make it defensive, and therefore negative, in its dealings with you. On the contrary, emphasise the positive aspects and this will encourage closer cooperation and interaction between all parties.

4.2 KNOW, TRAIN AND SUPPORT STAFF

4.2.1 Understand strengths and weaknesses

Selection of the project execution team should not be based solely on availability. It must take into consideration the way in which the potential team members are likely to interact with each other, with the other party's team and, in the case of an overseas contract, with the local population and other foreign nationals they are likely to encounter.

There is no hard and fast rule which can assist in this process; selection comes down to a mixture of common sense, experience and developing a good understanding of the people concerned. If you know your own team members but are unsure about the individual members of the other party's team then talk to as many people as you can that have had previous dealings with them and try to understand how they operate. With your knowledge of your own staff you should then be able to decide who has the necessary strengths to be included and who has weaknesses that make their inclusion undesirable.

4.2.2 Staff positioning

There may be a member of your staff who must be included in your project team for political or company reasons, but who might not relate well to the other party's team members. In this case consideration should be given to including an alternative person in the team who can act as a front. They might not be as familiar with specific issues if there is a dispute, but they will be able to put forward your team's position and deal with the other party's representatives diplomatically and effectively. In this way direct confrontation and the disadvantages that this could bring to the negotiation table would be avoided.

Not everyone possesses the skills of presentation and negotiation. It is perfectly understandable that the best person to research and prepare data might not be the best person to present those data to others. In time these skills might be acquired, but until that time arrives it is again best to use people who have the appropriate skills to make presentations to and negotiate with the other party.

4.2.3 Interpersonal skills

Interpersonal skills cannot really be taught effectively; they are either possessed or they are not. This does not mean that a person with poor interpersonal skills will never improve. On the contrary, with encouragement and suitably targeted, empathetic mentoring, improvements can be made, although there is no doubt that acquired skills are never as good as those that come naturally.

Improvement can also be encouraged through attendance of more formal courses designed for the specific purpose. Mentoring, however, is by far the most effective method. The person who wishes to acquire such skills will usually feel more comfortable watching and learning from a fellow team member in real life situations than being in a structured learning environment, where there might be more pronounced peer pressures from fellow students. Interpersonal skills are a personal issue and emotions come into play more than they would in a more technical or academic learning environment. Failure to impress in front of fellow students can damage self-belief, confidence and personal pride and could even act as a setback to the process of self improvement. Encouragement by a mentor within the same team, or at least within the same company, will produce far greater benefits.

4.2.4 Directional training in dispute management

Adequate directional training is an essential part of the whole dispute avoidance and management concept, and must be tailored to the particular aspect of the industry concerned. All dispute management staff must have a full and complete understanding of, and an acceptable level of knowledge in, the core competencies required of someone in their particular role.

The core competencies required of a dispute management team member are knowledge, skills and attitude.

4.2.4.1 Knowledge

Each member of the dispute management team must be able to demonstrate that they have an understanding of the characteristics of a dispute and how it manifests itself in a real life situation in a business context.

Subsidiary knowledge-based competencies must include the ability to understand:

- behavioural aspects of a dispute;
- cross-cultural consideration;
- casualties of dispute – loss of productivity, loss of morale etc.;
- different styles of dispute management;
- different strategies and their effects;
- basic motivational theories;
- power dynamics – imbalance of power and its impact on the parties;
- the complete dispute cycle, from emergence through to escalation, de-escalation, negotiation and settlement;
- differences between roles, responsibilities, processes and expected outcomes of mediation, adjudication, arbitration and negotiation;
- differences between compromise, cooperation, collaboration and consensus building;
- personality and dispute management styles, strengths and challenges.

4.2.4.2 Skills

Each dispute management team member must be able to demonstrate collaborative problem-solving skills in:

- active listening;
- formulating and expressing strategies defining the required outcomes;
- identifying underlying interests;
- identifying, developing and analysing options.

Subsidiary skill-based competencies must include the ability to:

- assess and manage interpersonal disputes;
- listen actively and responsively in order to facilitate understanding;
- understand the use and respective benefits of open and closed questions;
- demonstrate and identify different courses of action and analyse and understand the consequences and relative benefits of each, including actual and prospective costs and risks;
- identify the elements of a sustainable agreement on the dispute.

4.2.4.3 Attitude

Each dispute management team member must be able to demonstrate that they have a working knowledge of the ethical behaviour required of them in a collaborative dispute resolution context, including:

- neutrality;
- confidentiality;
- objectivity;
- respect of differences;
- honesty.

Subsidiary attitude-based competencies must include the ability to demonstrate knowledge of the basic negotiation rules of ethics and principles of practice, including:

- respect for all participating parties;
- professional accountability;
- freedom from bias;
- tolerance of different people and their different perspectives;
- the importance of gaining long-term credibility and trust based upon honesty;
- the importance of not personalising the dispute resolution process.

4.2.5 Danger signals

Watch out for warning signs that things are not going as smoothly as is desirable. Be aware of undercurrents in the day-to-day contact between the teams and establish at an early stage why they are there. It might be that there is a misunderstanding between members of the different teams that has not been discussed openly and resolved, leading to one party being frustrated or upset but unable to raise the issue for fear of upsetting relationships. With good communication channels and effective management such situations should not arise, but inevitably there will be occasions where their occurrence is unavoidable. The secret is to identify such situations and resolve them at the earliest opportunity.

Undercurrents might manifest themselves in a variety of ways, ranging from subtle (or not so subtle) hints made by one party to the other to a generally uncomfortable atmosphere when the parties meet which generates a sense or feeling that something is not quite right.

If the undercurrents are not recognised and dealt with early enough then the underlying causes will become more of an issue and attitudes will tend to polarise. The signs that things are getting more serious can include open rudeness by one party to the other, avoidance of face-to-face contact, an increasing tendency towards argumentativeness and the development of a blame culture. If these signs are ignored then it is inevitable that disputes will arise between the parties. Disputes that originate in this way are much more difficult to resolve because, as mentioned above, the parties will, during the incubation period, have polarised their thoughts. If the potential for a dispute had been recognised at an earlier stage the parties would have been more flexible in their approach to the issues concerned and an amicable resolution would have been more achievable.

4.2.6 Skill training

Earlier paragraphs have touched on training and education. It is recognised that not all skills can be taught; for example, in general terms we are born either with or without interpersonal skills. This does not, however, mean that they cannot be improved by training.

Technical and commercial skills can benefit hugely from effective training. Knowledge can be improved, and with knowledge comes a better understanding of the issues that the trainees are likely to come across in their day-to-day working environment. Attitudes can be improved to some extent, as can interpersonal skills, but these remain to a large degree dependent upon a person's own nature, upbringing and general approach to life. These are very difficult attributes to change and often the best we can hope for is that their negative aspects can be managed and controlled.

4.3 KNOW YOUR CONTRACT

This might sound too obvious to include here, yet it is surprising that, in practice, a significant deficiency in the level of contract awareness and understanding is often found in project execution teams.

To 'know your contract' in this context does not mean that you require the legal proficiency of a lawyer, but does require you to have an awareness of the obligations and responsibilities imposed by the contract. The team members responsible for preparing the tender bid must be fully aware of what those obligations and responsibilities are, together with the risks that their acceptance imposes. It is equally important that the project execution team is also fully aware of its obligations and responsibilities under the contract. It needs to be particularly aware of what decisions the tender preparation team made following on from its risk assessment, and how these are to be managed during project execution.

4.3.1 Ensure clear contract terms

The onus is on the tender preparation team to ensure that all the terms in the tender and contract documentation are clear, and that none could be open to misinterpretation, ambiguity, conflict, inconsistency or misunderstanding at a later date. Where any terms are considered unclear the tender preparation team should raise them with the employer and request clarification prior to submission of the bid. The clarifications received from the employer should be incorporated in the bid and, if the bid is successful, should then be incorporated in the contract so that there is no dispute during the execution of the contract works.

4.3.2 Assess commercial viability of contract

The tender preparation and evaluation teams are responsible for ensuring that the contract is commercially viable, based upon the terms and conditions which have been clarified in discussions between the employer and the contractor and incorporated into the bid documents. If there were any question as to the viability of the contract then it would be unwise to proceed with the bid unless the parties' higher management teams have made a policy decision to proceed at all costs for reasons outside the remit of the tender preparation and evaluation teams. These could reflect the employer's or contractor's long-term objectives in the area, in the particular work sector or with each other.

4.3.3 Understand the potentials for dispute

The tender preparation team should prepare a spreadsheet identifying each contract clause that might impose either an obligation or a responsibility on either party to the contract and where failure to conform to the clause would inevitably lead to dispute. It should then analyse what the risks and options are and identify the option that best fits in with the project objectives. If the tender bid is successful, this analysis will form part of the project package issued to the project execution team in order that the team members are aware of the basis upon which the contract was entered into and have a fuller understanding of what is expected of them.

When the project execution team receives the contract package it must study it in depth. This initial appraisal must not be restricted to senior management, although sensitive and confidential issues would have to be restricted in accordance with company policy. It is essential that each member of the project execution team at least understands the obligations and responsibilities that the contract imposes upon the contractor in the execution of its duties under the contract. It will be very beneficial to the project for each team member to have an overview of the effects of their particular obligations and responsibilities on the project as a whole.

If the project execution team fully understands the contract and the roles of the team members within the contract management structure, then the project risks will have already been reduced. If the rules imposed by the contract are both understood and applied properly then the chances of a dispute arising are also reduced.

4.3.4 Prepare schedule of contract requirements

Acquiring knowledge is only one part of the process; the application of that knowledge is equally important. The contract should be read thoroughly at the earliest opportunity. The commercial team should prepare a schedule of all the dates and time periods when or within which submissions must be made and actions taken. A typical schedule of submissions is suggested in Figure 4. A further schedule should be prepared identifying notice requirements, and a typical form is suggested in Figure 5. The process of preparing such schedules helps the team understand the various obligations and responsibilities imposed by the contract and the potential for disputes. The preparation of such schedules will also inevitably give rise to questions regarding the particular processes and timescales involved in the execution of the contract.

Preparing these schedules is another important part of the process; again, adhering to them is equally important. The project/commercial managers must drill their staff in the requirements of the contract as analysed in the prepared schedules (which should be made available to all team members) and in relation to each person's role within the project execution team. These roles, whether they be design, procurement,

Fig. 4 Schedule of Submissions (Typical Clauses)

Clause Number	Clause Heading	Item(s) to be Submitted	Term/Period for Submission
General Conditions of Contract			
8A.1	Performance Security	Contractor to furnish Employer with the performance security in the amount specified in the Special Conditions of Contract (SCC)	Within thirty (30) days after the Effective Date of Contract Commencement – to be discharged by Employer and returned to Contractor not later than thirty (30) days following issuance of the last Taking Over Certificate (TOC)
8B.1	Warranty Security	Contractor to submit to Employer Warranty Security for each Section in the amount specified in the SCC	Upon issuance of the TOC for each Section – to be discharged by Employer and returned to Contractor not later than thirty (30) days following expiry of the Warranty period for each relevant Section
12.1	Insurance	Contractor to submit identity of insurers and the form of the proposed policies to the Employer for approval	Before entering into policies
22.1	Subcontracts	Contractor to submit to Employer for its approval any addition or deletion from the list of subcontractors contained in Schedule E of the Contract	In sufficient time so as not to impede the progress of the works
21	Programmes and Progress	Contractor shall supply Employer with a preliminary schedule indicating key dates	Within twenty eight (28) days after the Effective Date
21	Programmes and Progress	Contractor shall supply Employer with three copies of the fully developed schedule to cover design, procurement and construction works	Within two (2) months after the Effective Date – schedule shall be analysed monthly thereafter or at such intervals as Employer determines
22	Meetings, Progress of Works and Progress Reports	Contractor shall submit to Employer a progress report of all the Works throughout the period of the Contract, including a photographic record of site activities and progress	Every four (4) weeks

continued. . .

Clause Number	Clause Heading	Item(s) to be Submitted	Term/Period for Submission
22	Meetings, Progress of Works and Progress Reports	Contractor's Site Representative shall submit a report to the Employer summarising site activities during the previous week and the main activities for the forthcoming week	Weekly
24	Drawings, Patterns and Samples	Contractor shall send four (4) copies of a list of all drawings and documents to be produced by Contractor under the Contract to the Employer	Within four (4) weeks after the Effective Date
24	Drawings, Patterns and Samples	Contractor shall maintain and submit to Employer a complete and updated drawing register	To be submitted monthly with the progress report
25	Procedure for Approval of Drawings	Employer shall advise the Contractor of the required data and documents with the due dates for the Environment Impact Assessment Report	Before the Effective Date
31	Operation, Maintenance and Repair Instructions	Contractor shall make available to Employer at Site hard copies and CD copies of the final operating, maintenance and repair instructions	At least one month before the programmed Taking Over date

engineering, commercial or project management, must be clearly defined and explained to all the team members to avoid any confusion or misunderstanding regarding the obligations and responsibilities established by the contract.

One of the most frustrating aspects of commercial management, whether on the employer's or the contractor's side, is the attitude that design, engineering and construction teams often have to commercial matters. It is often the case that the construction team's priorities in particular are clearly focused on completion of the project within the time agreed to in the contract. Construction teams often tend to disregard the niceties of commercial management where they consider that these might have a detrimental effect on their completion schedules. They can also disregard good commercial practices where they believe that to implement them could harm the relationships that they have built up with their employer's site management team.

Fig. 5 Schedule of Notice Requirements

Clause Number	Clause Heading/Title	Notice Requirement	Term/Period for Notice Submission	Comments
General Conditions of Contract				
23.2	Delays in the Contractor's Performance	Contractor to notify Employer if at any time the Contractor or its subcontractor(s) should encounter a delaying factor	Promptly when the delaying factor is encountered	Notice to include facts of delay, likely duration and causes. It is better to serve notice of delay and later withdraw it if circumstances change than not to serve notice at all
26.3	Force Majeure	Contractor to notify Employer when a Force Majeure condition arises	Promptly when situation arises (see SCC Clause 18.5 for precise period)	Notice must state the Force Majeure event or condition and its cause
27.1	Termination by the Employer	Employer shall issue a notice to the Contractor requiring it to make good and remedy any failure to carry out any of its obligations under the Contract	No period given	Remedy to be executed within a reasonable time but not later than sixty (60) days after receipt of Employer's notice. Any delay will give the Employer the right to terminate the Contract
27.2	Termination by the Employer	Employer must notify the Contractor of its intention to terminate the Contract	Thirty (30) days prior notice (except in the case of Contractor's bankruptcy, insolvency or liquidation etc. or Contractor giving a bribe or inducement etc., all as defined in 27.2(e) and (f)	
30	Resolution of Disputes	Either party may require that a dispute be referred for resolution by the formal mechanisms in the Special Conditions of Contract	At any time following the completion of thirty (30) days of formal amicable negotiations	The formal negotiations will need to be strictly defined with a start date and an end date thirty (30) days later so that this clause can be implemented
36.2	Extension of Time for Completion	Contractor shall submit to the Employer a notice of a claim for extension of time for completion	To be submitted as soon as reasonably practicable after the commencement of such event or circumstance	Notice to give particulars of the event or circumstance justifying such extension of time for completion

Good employer relationships are without doubt extremely important, but this must not be allowed to cloud good commercial judgment. The contract's clauses are there for the benefit of both parties. Failure to implement a clause might not only prejudice one party's chances of pursuing a claim at a later date but might also prevent the other party from making alternative arrangements to mitigate the claim at an appropriate time, such as opting for acceleration measures, thereby obviating the opportunity for dispute. In this respect, failure to serve a notice at the correct time could well prevent the employer from taking measures that would, in the long run, save it time or money. Rather than promoting good employer relationships, delaying a claim notice could in fact blight them. First-hand knowledge of the contract should prevent such errors of judgment occurring.

4.4 DO WHAT THE CONTRACT REQUIRES

4.4.1 Avoid making disputes where none exist

Contracts are the construction project equivalent of the football referee's rulebook. They are a set of rules that both sides have agreed to abide by while carrying out their respective roles and which make provision for suitable and appropriate sanctions to be applied should those rules be broken. There are also dispute resolution and appeals procedures that can be applied should either side feel aggrieved in any way.

It is very unlikely that any football player would take part in a major football match without first becoming familiar with the rules of the game, yet the parties to a construction contract frequently field 'players' on site who have no more than a cursory knowledge and understanding of the contract and even less knowledge of the remedies the other side can take against them should the contract rules be broken or ignored. This is a totally unacceptable situation.

The major players on a construction project should have more than a cursory understanding of the contract and should be coached in it before arriving on site. It is the duty and responsibility of each party to ensure that its team members understand their duties, obligations and rights under the contract. All team members must also understand the implications that events which apparently affect only their area of work can have on the big picture.

Once team members are aware of the contract as it affects them it is essential that they abide by it totally. This is a rule that must not be ignored. More disputes arise out of ignorance of or the misapplication of contractual requirements than any other cause. The contract may seem biased towards the interests of one party at the expense of the other, but this is of no relevance. The contract has been signed by both parties and each has to make the best of it. By taking its responsibilities seriously and by following the requirements of the contract to the letter, each party will give the other party confidence in its professionalism. This in turn will increase the level of trust that develops between them and minimise the likelihood of major disputes arising.

4.4.2 Serve notices in the manner and time required

The contract will require notices to be served by one party on the other in designated circumstances and in a designated manner. Strict adherence to these requirements will not only illustrate a party's professionalism, but will also preserve its rights under the contract. The contract may well say that notices have to be served within a specific time period following the events to which they relate, and that failure to do so will negate a party's right to claim at a later date – i.e. making serving a notice a condition precedent to a party having the right to have its claim accepted for review at a later date. This type of clause is becoming more popular, and failure to observe it causes many claims to fail on the grounds that they were made out of time. The wording of such clauses can vary considerably. If ignored, some clauses, particularly those containing the 'condition precedent' wording mentioned above, will be fatal to your chances of submitting a later claim. Some, however, may just be vague enough to give you a chance of recovering from your failure to make a timely submission. This element of doubt will be eliminated if the requirements of the contract are followed in each and every case.

If the contract is followed to the letter and each notice is served within the time period specified, to the person and at the address given in the contract, then the chances of a procedural dispute arising at a later date are eliminated. This in turn makes a positive contribution to the process of settling the subject matter of the notice. If notices are served on time then both parties have the opportunity of discussing the issues concerned and reaching an agreement while the subject matter is fresh in their minds. Very often the party upon whom the notice is served has not thought the issue through adequately, and the receipt of a notice, which shows how the issue affects time and/or cost on the project, can serve to focus its mind more clearly on the issues. This may result in the original instruction being modified in some way, or even withdrawn.

The contractor may be of the opinion that an instruction issued by the employer will cause both time and cost impacts to the project. If it serves notice to the employer to this effect, possibly requesting a change order to formalise the situation, the employer will have the opportunity of reviewing its position. It may decide to proceed as per the original instruction and enter into negotiations with the contractor on the time and cost impacts, or it might decide to withdraw the instruction and search for other less contentious means of achieving its objectives. Alternatively, the employer may be prepared to accept additional costs but will not allow additional time, in which case it might discuss methods of acceleration with the contractor.

If issues are not brought to the employer's attention at an early enough stage then the opportunity for the employer to propose mitigating actions, such as initiating acceleration, will be lost. This would place the employer in a difficult situation. For example, the employer may have instructed work to be carried out but had not realised the need for authorised measures that would have minimised the time and cost disruptions resulting from its instruction. The dispute, which would be inevitable in such a situation, could have been easily avoided if the contractor had abided by the requirements of the contract and served its notice on the employer at the appropriate time.

Notices do not only relate to confirmation of instructions: they may be required to confirm when certain information is required, when certain milestones have been reached and when laws, regulations, standards etc. have been modified, changed or introduced. Failure to comply with notice provisions will decrease a party's chances of introducing the issues concerned into claims at later stages in the project, and will accordingly increase the chances of disputes arising on these issues.

4.4.3 Do not act without proper documentation

Construction teams on site frequently go against good commercial practice by agreeing to implement the employer's verbal instructions without first obtaining written confirmation. This can lead to a number of contentious issues: whether the work was actually instructed, whether it was an instruction to carry out additional work, whether it was intended as variation work, whether or not such work would be paid for and, if so, whether a quotation was required, whether payment would be based on measured rates, or whether the work should be recorded on daywork. Each of these alternative scenarios can give rise to a dispute unless clearly agreed to in writing before the work is implemented.

The only exception to the need for a written confirmation is if the additional or varied work has been instructed by the employer on health and safety grounds, or in respect of some other emergency, where the verbal instruction's prior confirmation in writing is a physical or legal impossibility. In such cases it would be necessary to commence the work immediately while at the same time confirming the instruction back to the employer, stating that a lack of response would be taken as deemed approval of the actions being taken.

Many contractors are wary of upsetting the employer during the critical stages of a contract and so as a matter of policy tend to do whatever the employer requests them to do. Only later do they question the commercial aspects of the instruction, when the additional work has been completed and the contract is coming to an end. By trying to avoid a dispute with the employer they are in fact leaving themselves open to a potentially greater dispute by delaying discussion. If the matter is raised at the time of the instruction the employer is given the opportunity to think twice as to whether in fact it is prepared to pay extra for the additional work or whether, on reconsidering its position, it would prefer to cancel the instruction and maintain the status quo. If discussion on the issue concerned is left until the work has been completed and the employer then confirms that it had no intention of paying for it as additional work, the contractor finds itself in a dispute situation. The options open to the contractor are to proceed with the dispute under whatever dispute resolution provisions are contained within the contract or to bite the bullet and accept that it has to bear the cost itself as a result of its earlier reticence.

Dispute avoidance is the preferable option for both parties, and ignoring an issue until the contract close-out stage helps no one. The sooner a potential dispute is brought to everyone's attention the sooner it can be laid to rest, hopefully without significant dispute resolution measures having to be implemented.

Generally, contracts have a clause that gives the contractor the power, and indeed obliges the contractor, to apply to the employer for a change order. This will apply each time the contractor considers that an instruction made by the employer or a change of circumstance beyond the contractor's control warrants the issuance by the employer of a change order. This clause is there for a purpose, and is actually for the benefit of both the employer and the contractor. It gives the contractor the opportunity of recouping the additional costs and/or time resulting from an employer's instruction or change of relevant circumstance. For the employer it provides the opportunity to review its intentions as regards the instruction and, if it decides it should stand and be confirmed by a change order, then it is able to formalise its instruction and maintain its other rights under the contract which may otherwise have been lost, diluted or become the subject of later disputes.

Such a case could in theory occur if a verbal instruction issued by the employer is acted upon by the contractor without the benefit of an official change order, and the contractor subsequently claims 'time at large' due to the contract period not having been adjusted to account for time taken to execute the additional work (assuming that there is no other contractual mechanism in place whereby the contractor can claim an extension of time). This would have the potential of leaving the employer bearing additional costs for the extended period and losing its contractual right to claim liquidated damages from the contractor. The chances of such a situation occurring are slim, although I recently experienced such a situation on a project in Italy where there were no extension of time mechanisms in the contract relating to a delay caused by the employer and the Italian Civil Code's equivalent of 'time at large' had to be brought into play.

4.5 IDENTIFY AREAS OF POTENTIAL DISPUTE

4.5.1 Anticipate potential dispute situations

The process of potential dispute identification starts at the tender bid stage, when the pre-tender risk assessment is carried out. The risk assessment should have highlighted all the potential disputes that could be contemplated at that time. These should have been placed into a risk register, identifying which risks were deemed acceptable, which were to be passed on, which were to be insured against and which needed to be managed effectively during the project execution stage.

The risk register should be updated on a regular basis during the course of the contract. Progress on the management of previously identified risk items should be defined and new items added as and when they are identified. The risk register must be under the control of one person, although contributions will be required from each section or division involved in the project. One person must take overall responsibility for the risk register, but may assign this responsibility to a risk manager and/or individual section heads. The risk register must be updated on a weekly or monthly basis depending upon the size and nature of the project concerned, and must be copied to all relevant senior managers. In this way the project execution team is kept up to date with potential dispute issues and has the opportunity to discuss them with the other party, hopefully defusing any situations before a formal dispute arises.

4.5.2 Potentially contentious issues exist in every contract

However well a contract document is drafted there will be clauses that will give rise to disputes, either in their interpretation or in their application. As the project proceeds circumstances will change, and clauses that were previously considered innocuous will be viewed from a different perspective. These will need to be discussed with the other party if disputes are to be avoided.

There will be always be issues that could develop into disputes if not handled correctly or not discussed adequately and in due time. A trained eye will be able to identify them based on current knowledge, past experience, or a combination of both. It is good practice to maintain a register of dispute situations that have been experienced on previous projects or which are known to occur in the industry, in the particular location of the project, or in projects of a similar nature. For example, local knowledge might suggest that certain by-laws or local labour practices could cause problems if not properly understood and dealt with in the appropriate manner. Access issues frequently present problems, as do interface issues concerned with the employer and/or other contractors carrying out work on the same site, albeit in different contractual relationships.

All issues that are thought to have dispute potential should be entered on the risk register and monitored closely. Each issue should be discussed with the other party at the earliest opportunity so that a potential dispute can be defused before it develops into something more serious.

In addition to the risk register it is wise to keep a record of each identified potential dispute situation as it develops: a typical record sheet is suggested in Figure 6. This should record the chronology of events, including all correspondence, minutes of meetings etc. where the concerned issue has been discussed. It should also identify the strengths and weaknesses of each party's actions and reactions, whether they were made in a timely fashion or whether they were delayed unduly. This will be a very useful document when the issue becomes a dispute and dispute settlement procedures are invoked. By that time staff changes may have taken place and memories will have become clouded by subsequent events, and the people deputed to resolve the dispute will need all the help they can get to recognise the exact circumstances under which the dispute developed.

4.5.3 Plan to avoid potentially contentious issues developing into disputes

Once a potential dispute has been identified, included on the risk register and notified to the other party, attention must be given to how it can best be prevented from escalating into a formal dispute.

The first step is to establish what your own goals and objectives are and how you would like to see the issue resolved. You will then need to give some thought to how best to open discussions with the other party to ensure that your goals and objectives can be achieved. No doubt the other party will have slightly different thoughts from yours. The contractor will want to ensure that all its additional time and costs will be recovered and the employer will want to minimise its exposure to both.

Deciding the correct strategy is an art in itself and will come from experience gained through encountering similar situations on previous projects. The main thrust at this time should be directed at gaining the confidence and trust of the other party, such that it understands and sympathises with the position you find yourself in and sees the need to cooperate with you in your attempts to find a mutually acceptable solution without allowing a dispute to develop.

4.5.4 Be realistic about acceptable level of risk

In the risk assessment, each risk will have been allocated ratings showing how likely it is to become an issue of concern and its acceptability. Some risks can be accepted totally, some can be passed on to the employer, subcontractors or suppliers, others could be covered by insurances, bonds or the like.

Fig. 6 Potential Dispute Issues – Chronology of Events

ID	Date	From	To	Title	Ref	Subject Matter	In Reply to:	Strengths	Weaknesses	Comments
A. Demolition Work (Start Date)										
A1	26.09.07	C	S/C	Letter of Intent	SC-L-089	Letter of Intent for Demolition Work				
A2	28.09.07	C	E	Demolition S/C	Emp-L-103	Confirmation that subcontractor has been appointed	Con-16008	Timely appointment in accordance with Contract schedule	Full subcontract documentation not available	Complete documentation as soon as possible
A3	04.10.07	E	C	Access to Site	Con-16217	Confirms access to site now available as required by the Contract	Emp-L-103	Access made available in accordance with Contract schedule	No construction permit issued by E at that time	Serve notice on E claiming delay caused by late issuance of permit schedule
A4	05.10.07	C	E	Commence Demolition Work	Emp-L-109	Requesting two weeks notice before commencement of demolition work – needed for mobilisation of plant and labour	Con-16105	Construction permit not yet issued, no work can start before it is received by C	No notice period in Contract	Two weeks notice requirement confirmed and agreed to at weekly meeting on 05.08.07
A5	07.10.07	E	C	Commence Demolition Work	Con-16500	Requesting copies of S/C agreements before E able to issue instruction to commence work	Emp-L-109	Contract does not oblige C to copy S/C agreements to E	To refuse could annoy E and delay works	In order to avoid dispute agree to copy unpriced agreement to E
A6	11.10.07	C	E	Commence Demolition Work	Emp-L-131	Puts responsibility for delays in design approval on to E	Con-16217	Previous C letters and weekly meeting minutes suggested that design delay situation was E's responsibility	C didn't actually serve notice on E as required by the Contract	Site management previously reluctant to submit formal claim notice in fear of upsetting E
A7	12.10.07	N/A	N/A	Minutes of Weekly Meeting	MOM	C must have Health and Safety (H&S) Plans approved by E before commencing demolition works	N/A	H&S plans already submitted to E for approval, awaiting this for 5 weeks to date	C hasn't chased approval or notified E that late approval would delay project work	Serve notice of delay on E claiming delay caused by E's late approval of H&S plans and drawings

Legend: C = Contractor; E = Employer; S/C = Subcontractor

Both parties must be realistic about how much risk they are prepared to accept. It will be impossible to avoid all risk and each party should establish what degree of risk is acceptable before entering into negotiations with the other party. There is little point in attempting to negotiate a compromise if a party's principal objective is to absolve itself from all risk: that would be a waste of time and effort and would leave the other party with a distinctly negative impression. This in turn would prove detrimental to future negotiations since this negativity would precede that party into the new forum.

4.5.5 Have escape strategies in place for each stage

Each party will have established its aims and objectives and set its negotiation strategy before commencing negotiations. The various aims and objectives of the parties will inevitably be at variance, otherwise the issue would not have reached this stage.

Such variances are to be expected in negotiation situations. Each party should prepare several scenarios that can be called into play depending upon what strategies the other parties adopt and what route the negotiations take. The fact that a party has obviously thought out the issues concerned and is able to show flexibility in its approach to the potential dispute will go in its favour. The other party will see that it is making a positive effort to resolve the issues and will be encouraged by its willingness to consider compromising its own position. This will make the achievement of the principal goal, the avoidance of a dispute, more attainable.

4.6 AVOID BACKLASH SITUATIONS

4.6.1 People resent being forced to do something against their will

It is a fact of life that people have an in-built aversion to doing something against their will. This is the same in business as it is in our day-to-day lives and we need to be constantly aware of this, particularly so when we are in a potential dispute situation. If you are facing a party who is determined to have its own way come what may then you will have to employ all the tact and diplomacy that you are capable of in order to avoid a dispute situation. Persuasion can come in many forms and the means that you decide to employ will depend upon the precise issue that you are facing and the personalities concerned.

This is another situation that highlights the benefits of getting to know your colleagues, whether they are part of your team or another party's. If you know their good and bad points, their attitudes to work in general and to their company in particular, and if you can gain some understanding of what makes them tick, you will be in a stronger position when a situation such as this occurs. If you can use your diplomatic skills to direct their enthusiasm towards the goals that you are trying to achieve then you will be better placed to gain their agreement. They should be made to feel that they have contributed towards and have played a part in the decision-making process that resulted in the solution of a contentious issue.

4.6.2 Level of resentment increases when pressure is seen as illegitimate

There is legitimate pressure and illegitimate pressure. It is legitimate to use the contract terms and conditions to apply pressure on the other party to meet its obligations and responsibilities under that contract. It is illegitimate to apply pressures that cannot be supported by the contract terms and conditions, such as withholding monies rightly due until other unrelated work is carried out, or preventing access to one section of a site until another section has been completed. These are pressures often applied by employers to expedite the works. However, such pressures are seen as intimidating and nurture resentment by the party being pressurised. This resentment might not surface at the time, or even in relation to the particular issue which has given rise to it, but it might play a dominant role in the future relationship between the parties should a dispute situation arise in respect of another aspect of the works. It is irrelevant that there might be contractual remedies available to the party being pressurised, such as claiming interest on withheld monies, as these do little to ease the overall feelings of resentment that such action will inevitably encourage. Avoid applying illegitimate pressure and endeavour to be open and honest in your dealings at all times. There is no need for such actions unless the contract has been badly prepared and you have no other means of urging the other party to meet its obligations and responsibilities.

4.6.3 Illegitimate actions include those considered excessive or unnecessary

Withholding monies otherwise due as a means of pressurising the other party to expedite its performance of the works would be deemed excessive, particularly if by having monies withheld the suffering party was placed in a position whereby it could not finance the work that the other party hoped to expedite. The suffering party might not have sufficient financial resources available to pay its subcontractors or purchase materials necessary to expedite the works. This restriction of cash flow could have serious adverse effects on the completion of the works. Such action would be bound to end up as a dispute. Dispute avoidance in such a case will rely upon either the instigator of the illegitimate pressure opting instead to enforce any remedies available to it under the contract, or on the delaying party to agree to expedite its works before the need for pressure of any kind becomes necessary.

4.6.4 Explore all negotiation avenues before commencing ADR

It is important that the parties should explore all avenues of negotiation before invoking ADR clauses or filing lawsuits against another party. As soon as such clauses are invoked or legal action commenced, the positions taken by the parties will inevitably become more polarised and the chances of an amicable settlement being reached will be diminished significantly. In addition, the parties will immediately start incurring significant additional costs related to the ADR or court actions. It is always worth spending a little extra time on negotiation in the hope that an amicable solution can be reached.

4.6.5 Reduce backlash effect

Illegitimate pressures will do no one any good in the long run and anything that can be done to avoid their instigation should be considered. In the example given previously, where monies otherwise due are withheld, the potential backlash effects of this are enormous. If the party upon whom the pressure is applied has, as a result of these pressures, insufficient financial resources to complete its works, then it could well go into liquidation and the contract terminated. The lost time that this pressure was intended to recover would then seem insignificant in comparison with the time lost going through the termination procedures and appointing a new contractor to take over and complete the works. In addition to the time considerations, it is highly likely that any completion contract would prove far more expensive than the original contract. The result for the party who imposed the illegitimate pressure would be far greater time and cost impacts than if it had not applied the pressure. This backlash effect could have been avoided if the parties had sat down and negotiated their differences in an open manner. It is highly likely that a solution could have been reached, involving perhaps an acceleration payment being made to the contractor. This would have imposed lower financial burden on the employer than would the termination and re-appointment option brought about by its application of illegitimate pressure.

4.7 EFFECTIVE COMMUNICATION

4.7.1 Open lines of communication

Communication is arguably the most important weapon in the fight against the proliferation of construction disputes. Clear lines of communication must be open between people who rely on one another to get work done. It is therefore imperative that one of the first actions of the project team at the start of a project is to set up official lines of communication. It is not sufficient only to define lines of communication between the respective project managers. Each head of section or discipline should also direct communication with their opposite number.

Some nationalities and cultures impose their own restrictions on communication between individuals. As an example, under the Japanese system of management everything is decided in a 'committee' structure and individual communication is frowned upon unless specifically authorised by the committee. Due regard has to be taken of this when planning a project execution strategy. I have been engaged by the Japanese on several projects and frequently an element of my brief, albeit unofficial, has been to establish direct links with the employer and its team, which the Japanese were barred from doing themselves by national and company culture. My role as a communication channel has always proved effective and has contributed to the avoidance of several disputes.

Unofficial approaches are equally important as official ones, and equal attention should be given to establishing unofficial lines of communication wherever possible. This is a route which should find favour with both management and employees in a system of management where official communication is restricted. A typical method of establishing unofficial lines would be to maximise the opportunities provided in a social context, such as golf, tennis or any other limited participant sport, dining or even visiting the pub. Others could involve joining a local community-based group such as Rotary, Round Table or Lions Club, or any other similar grouping where opposite numbers could share an interest and build up a rapport that would stand them in good stead in their working relationships. This works in whatever country the project is located and is equally effective whether your opposite number is a fellow expat who needs your support in an unfamiliar environment, or a country national with enthusiasm for sharing their country's culture and heritage with you.

4.7.2 Poor communication leads to lack of cooperation

Where the parties, and more particularly their representatives, fail to have adequate lines of communication in place there will inevitably be misunderstandings and the likelihood of disputes developing will be increased. Often, lack of communication gives the false impression that the other party has a negative attitude towards cooperation. Cooperation and communication are possibly the two most important factors that contribute to a successful project. Without either there is every chance of the parties becoming embroiled in disputes. There can be communication without cooperation, but there cannot be cooperation without communication, making communication the single most important factor to be addressed at the commencement of the project. This does not even mean waiting until the contract has been awarded. The first impressions of how the parties will integrate and cooperate are made at the bid and negotiation stages and very often relationships are formed before the contract is signed. However, if the bid and negotiation stages have not been adequately managed, the parties have a second chance once the contract has been awarded and the project team is assembled. Hopefully, any negative impressions given at the bid/negotiation stages can be overcome by the project team. Where the parties are aware of such negativity, effort must be put into ensuring that this negativity is not carried forward to the project execution stage.

4.7.3 Ensure regular reporting and discussion between the parties

A simple way of initiating a culture of good communication is to establish regular meetings, both formal and informal, between the parties' representatives. This will include the weekly or monthly progress meetings that are likely to be required under the contract, together with individual departmental or section meetings, such as between the civil, mechanical, electrical, architectural, QA/QC, safety and other relevant groups. It is important that minutes of the meetings are taken, agreed and circulated to those present and to all those who have an interest in their content. As well as serving as a record of discussions held and decisions reached (in case of later disputes), the minutes will further promote communication and cooperation between the parties.

4.7.4 Ensure the buy in of the site team

Project execution site teams, including those of both the employer and the contractor, tend to make the completion of the contract works on time their priority, and often neglect to give the desired level of attention to either the contract or commercial management aspects of the project. They are not always as keen as they should be to confirm verbal instructions, put forward change order requests and question employer decisions. To overcome this it is essential that the meeting and reporting procedures outlined above are put into place from the outset and that the project site teams 'buy into' this approach to contract and commercial management. Without their full cooperation the chances of disputes arising at a later date are significantly increased.

4.7.5 Look for signs of disputes developing and try to nip them in the bud

One of the secrets of effective contract and commercial management is the ability to identify a possible dispute situation before it has the chance to become established. This can be identified in the tone of correspondence, for example, particularly where it can be seen to be changing for the worse as the project progresses. It can also be seen in the verbal attitudes and body language apparent at the weekly or monthly meetings. Often the regular participants are the last to notice these changes. An outside observer has more chance of identifying potential disputes and changes in attitude than a person who has been directly involved in the development and responses to correspondence and who has attended the meetings on a regular basis. This is another reason for communications, including correspondence and minutes of meetings, to be circulated beyond those involved at site level on a day-to-day basis, so that fresh pairs of eyes can identify when things start going awry.

4.7.6 Beware of talking to one party in dispute behind another's back

Effective communication is dependent on developing an atmosphere of mutual trust and cooperation. This atmosphere can be destroyed if one party discovers that it was not included in communications with another party on a matter that concerns it. This identifies a third vital ingredient of good contract administration in addition to communication and cooperation, and that is inclusion. It is essential that all parties feel that their importance to the success of the project is recognised and that they are included in all discussions that directly or indirectly affect them. If there are logistical or time restrictions on a party's inclusion then at the very least it should be informed in good time of intended discussions, be given the opportunity of attending and be informed of the outcomes. If discussions take place without its knowledge and without the results being transmitted to it, then the vital element of trust has been lost.

4.7.7 Establish personal relationships

It cannot be emphasised enough that the development of good personal relationships between opposite numbers in the various parties' organisations, including any consultants, subcontractors or the like working for them, can play a massive part in the overall strategy of dispute avoidance. This has nothing to do with the giving or receiving of favours, but has everything to do with developing an atmosphere of trust and cooperation and creating open lines of communication.

If a potential dispute situation is recognised at an early enough point in time the parties should, if they have developed good personal relationships, be able to discuss it openly and freely, at least as far as their relative positions under the contract allow them to (i.e. as long as they are not breaching any conflict of interest rules or ethical considerations). The secret is to resolve the potential dispute before it reaches a higher or wider level of management, where the flexibility to make such an agreement is not always so readily available.

4.7.8 Question and break stereotypes

The construction industry is just like any other, in that those involved in it have stereotypical views of the various players involved. Contractors believe that all employers are out to take advantage of them, employers think the same about contractors, as do the contractor's subcontractors and suppliers. Contractors have no doubt that the employer's consultant will naturally side with the employer should a dispute arise.

The only way to break this attitude is to build up professional and personal relationships as described above. It is essential that an atmosphere of mutual trust is established at the earliest opportunity. This will contribute to the process of questioning whether the other party, or at least its representatives, really fits in to the stereotypical mould expected for them. Once the stereotypes have been dispelled and it is realised that all parties really have the same basic objective, i.e. completing the project on time and within budget, cooperation becomes that bit easier. Of course there is always one project where the stereotype rules, and in such a case it is more difficult to practise dispute avoidance – note 'more difficult', certainly not 'impossible'.

4.7.9 Communication – accuracy and respectfulness

Good communication channels contribute significantly to the establishment of a dispute-free project; however, they are not enough on their own. Having set up good communication channels, the next step is to ensure that those channels are used positively and not negatively. This is entirely dependent upon the quality of information that is allowed to pass through those channels, the manner in which it is disseminated and the attitude and enthusiasm of the users.

Data and information of any kind communicated to another party must be clear, concise and accurate if high levels of trust are to be maintained. Trust diminishes when fault can be found in the data or information transmitted. This can lead to questions being asked as to whether such inaccuracies or inconsistencies were introduced by accident or whether they were included with the deliberate intention of misleading.

The manner of transmission is equally important. Communication between the parties must be made in a timely manner and must at all times show respect for the other party and for its opinions, views and positions taken. This issue links with the stereotype considerations mentioned earlier, and is particularly important in relation to communication from employer to contractor and contractor to subcontractor. Stereotyping assumes that the employer considers itself to be superior to the contractor and that the contractor considers itself superior to the subcontractor. In practice each party must respect the relative standing and importance of the other, since each has an important part to play in the success of the project and each is necessary in its own way. The manner in which communication is handled can prove the preconceptions to be false, to the benefit of both the parties and the project.

4.7.10 Shuttle diplomacy

Shuttle diplomacy can be defined 'as an attempt to make peace between two groups of people, who refuse to meet and talk to each other, by meeting each group separately and travelling between them'.[1]

Generally, holding separate meetings with the parties involved in a potential or active dispute is not to be looked upon favourably. However, occasions arise where it is impossible to do otherwise. Since communication between the parties is still the most effective means of resolving a dispute without recourse to arbitration or litigation, there is scope in construction projects for the application of shuttle diplomacy. This will usually entail the use of a third party, preferably someone involved in the project at a different level, or someone appointed specifically to carry out this task, who will serve as an intermediary or mediator between the parties who are refusing to talk.

I have recently been involved in a dispute within a consortium in which two of the consortium partners had technical functions and one had purely administrative functions. The two technical members disagreed on a number of issues. The consortium agreement allowed for such disputes and designated the consortium leader to carry out what was in effect shuttle diplomacy as a first step in attempting to resolve the dispute. Unfortunately, in this particular case the consortium leader was found to have bias against one of the technical partners in dispute and so his findings were discounted, which shows that even when the mechanics are in place, success is not inevitable. Similar situations could come about by mutual agreement and need not be set out in the contract or other formal agreement between the parties.

4.7.11 Enhance communication skills

If employees have poor communication skills, their productivity will suffer because they will be unable to influence, persuade and negotiate effectively with parties at all levels. Good communication skills come naturally to some people, in others they have to be taught. In both cases the skills can be enhanced by properly focused training. Unfortunately, however, it is rare to find a company that takes communication skills seriously enough to provide such training for its staff. More often than not the company will merely prepare a standard contract management manual defining procedures to be followed in a number of standard situations and expect employees to abide by it, hoping that this will adequately cover any failings an individual employee might have as regards communication skills. This leads to a situation where there is a rigid adherence to procedural communication and no natural communication between the parties. In fact it is very often the case that the manuals are so precise in the approaches they demand that they tend to restrict employees' natural abilities to communicate on a one-to-one basis.

A contract management manual can by all means include official procedures for inter-party communication, defining agreed channels, reference numbering systems, instructions for dissemination of copies etc., but it should not restrict opportunities for direct and natural communication between individuals. This cannot be set down in the form of strict procedures but should be allowed to develop naturally, albeit with a little encouragement from management. If employees are considered lacking in the necessary skills then these should be provided either as a line management responsibility or by the use of outside specialist consultants.

4.7.12 New leader briefings

Communication starts within your own company. When the project team has been appointed, usually some time after the negotiations have been concluded, and the contract has been signed, the pre-contract team must pass on all relevant information to the project manager and commercial manager responsible for the execution of the project.

This will include minutes of pre-contract meetings and memos covering all aspects of discussions between the parties during the bid preparation and negotiation stages, the risk analysis and/or risk register updated as of the date of contract signature, and all correspondence between the parties. In addition to these formal elements the pre-contract team should also brief the project execution team on the nature of the personalities representing the other party with whom they have been in discussions, including their attitudes towards the project and to their opposite numbers, the perceived objectives of the other party, and any idiosyncrasies that the project team should be aware of.

The handover stage from pre-contract team to project execution team is a vital stage in the project. There must be full cooperation, coordination and communication between the teams in order to avoid later misunderstandings, both internally and in front of the other party. If the other party can see that there has been a full and comprehensive transfer of information to the project team, and that the project execution team is aware of the full background to the project, this will further help to build up confidence and trust, which can only be to the ultimate benefit of the both the parties and the project.

4.8 ACTIVE LISTENING

4.8.1 Basics of active listening

You must have the ability to listen attentively if you are to avoid disputes and misunderstandings and perform effectively in your particular sphere of work. This is particularly true in contracting, and even more so if the projects you are involved in are international as you will also have the added complications of linguistic and cultural differences to take account of. Active listening should be a positive state and every effort must be made to avoid giving a negative impression to the speaker. The first rule is that you should listen to understand, not to agree or disagree.

People generally speak at around 100 to 175 words per minute but they can listen at 600 to 800 words a minute. This means that only a part of your mind is paying attention to what is being said and so it is easy for your thoughts to drift to more pressing areas. Through practising active listening, using body language and focus skills, the chances of mind drift are minimised. An effective way of reducing mind drift is to repeat to yourself the words you are hearing. This not only focuses the mind on the speaker but reinforces your ability to remember what has been said.

Factors which inhibit active listening, and which must therefore be overcome, include:

*   self-consciousness;

*   emotion regarding the subject matter;

*   planning what to say next;

*   entering into judgment of the content and/or the speaker;

*   tiredness.

Practising active listening forces the listener to be attentive to what is being said: 'Research has found that on average we spend 45% of our time listening, 30% reading and 9% writing. If this is correct then it reinforces the importance of active listening'.[2]

4.8.2 Focus on speaker

The speaker must be the most important person in your life while he or she is speaking, and you must give off positive vibrations to this effect. You must focus your attention on the speaker and nothing else. Do not carry on with other work, read a totally disconnected document or check the time at frequent intervals as if you really need to be somewhere else. All of these give the speaker the impression that you are not really interested in what they have to say, and this in turn fuels misunderstandings and, later, disputes.

Ask pertinent questions on the topic being discussed. Do not wander off the subject, as this will imply either that you were not listening to what was being said or that the subject matter didn't really interest you at that time. Questions should be 'open questions', including the words 'tell me more' or 'what made you say that?'. Open questions cannot be answered by a simple 'yes' or 'no', and so give the speaker the opportunity of expanding on their thoughts and clarifying particular points you are unclear on. It is equally supportive for questions to be 'reflective', in which you state in your own words what you believe the speaker has said. This type of question shows that you have been listening and are asking for confirmation that you have understood what has been said.

Questions asked while the speaker is still talking can help the discussion. They can encourage the speaker to go into greater depth or to expand the boundaries of the topic of discussion. These questions should be asked at natural breaks in the speaker's dialogue and should not be intrusive such that they break the speaker's train of thought.

By focusing on the speaker and asking appropriate questions at appropriate times, the levels of understanding and trust between yourself and the speaker will increase. This will help prevent future misunderstandings and disputes developing, both on the subject matter concerned and, hopefully, more generally. Your questions will also show the other listeners that you are on top of the situation and they will see that you are developing a relationship with the speaker. This might then encourage them to be more attentive and to ask questions of their own, further increasing the dialogue between the parties, which in turn will make a positive contribution to the avoidance of misunderstandings and disputes.

4.8.3 Repeat what you hear

When it is your turn to speak in response, it is a good idea to repeat the salient points raised by the speaker. Starting your repetition of the salient points with the words 'If I have understood you correctly…' gives a positive message to the speaker that you are really trying hard to grasp the message they were trying to get across to you. This approach not only indicates to the speaker that you were in fact actively paying attention to what was being said, but also helps verify that what you believe you heard was in fact what the speaker intended you to hear. If your repeated summation of what was said is in any way flawed then the speaker has the opportunity of correcting you, which both helps you in your understanding and gives the speaker confidence that you have actually understood the points being made.

Through repeating the salient points in front of the speaker and through giving the speaker the opportunity of agreeing or disagreeing with your summation, the chances of a dispute arising on the subject concerned are minimised.

4.8.4 Interpret speaker's feelings

Interpreting the speaker's feelings enables you to judge the level of intensity with which their views are held. Responding by saying 'You seem quite upset about…' indicates both that you heard what the speaker was saying and that you understood the underlying message the speaker was trying to get across. If the speaker confirms that your observation was correct, they would know that you understood both the substance of and the emotion behind what was being said. This will further enhance the levels of confidence and trust that the speaker will have in you and will contribute significantly to the avoidance of disputes on the current or subsequent subject of discussion.

4.8.5 Understand relationship of body language to active listening

Positive body language is relatively easy to learn, understand and put into practice and sends messages confirming or denying both attention and interest. The essential elements that we should all apply to day-to-day contact relationships, not just in a construction project context, are:

- Make positive eye contact by looking at the speaker directly – avoiding eye contact gives the impression that you are either not interested in what is being said, are bored or have more important things you should be doing or more important people to be with.

- Present a square, open posture towards the speaker indicating that you are not trying to hide, are not bored and are in fact keen to hear what is being said.

- If possible lean forward towards the speaker, again showing that there is nothing more important to you at that point in time than actively listening to what is being said.

- Appear alert, do not yawn or look bored – if you are actually tired or bored then stifle this by sipping from a glass of water. This refreshes you and gives you a few moments to gather your thoughts and re-focus your attention on the speaker.

- Nod in agreement when you understand or agree with a particular point and smile at appropriate times, indicating to the speaker that you have been paying attention and that what the speaker has been saying has had some positive effect on you – there is time to give alternative opinions after the speaker has completed their part in the discussion.

- Avoid bodily or facial expressions that could imply negative judgment on what the speaker has been saying. Again there is time to give alternative opinions when it is your turn to speak.

4.9 PROCEDURAL GUIDANCE

4.9.1 Prevention treats the condition

For dispute avoidance to be practised effectively management must have in-depth knowledge of what types of condition create disputes. Only then can they introduce dispute avoidance measures particular to a specific contract and to the specific parties involved. If you can treat the condition that is likely to create a dispute then the chances of a dispute arising are removed or at least minimised.

Spotting the danger signs is a skill that cannot really be taught. It is possible to give pointers that will guide you along the right route but there is no real substitute for experience. The signs of a dispute brewing are often overlooked. However, if you know what signs you are looking for it is easy to spot them at an early enough stage to enable you to take the necessary action. Signs could include tensions within your own team or between your team and that of the other party or parties involved in the contract. Meetings could be developing into arenas in which the respective parties merely express their conflicting opinions rather than discuss the options openly with each other. The tone of emails and letters between the parties might be changing from friendly to aggressive or defensive, and interaction between the parties outside working hours might become strained or might even cease altogether. These are all changes that an effective manager should notice before attitudes become entrenched.

4.9.2 Establish management procedures

One of the themes flowing through this book is that nothing can replace good communication and record keeping as the principal tools for the avoidance and settlement of disputes. All parties must establish procedures within their own management teams that ensure their management team members are playing to the same rules and understand the aims and objectives of the company and its intentions for the contract.

These management procedures should, wherever possible, be integrated with those of the other parties, at least in broad terms. The parties must establish dispute management procedures that can be implemented whenever the team members deem it appropriate or when management observes the early warning signs that indicate a dispute may be developing.

4.9.3 Encourage healthy discussion

Many disputes arise as a direct result of team members not having either the ability or the inclination to enter into healthy and open discussions with their opposite numbers on issues which are, or could become, contentious. One of the roles of management that is so often overlooked is the creation of an atmosphere where healthy discussion is encouraged. This can be achieved by conducting formal/semi-formal 'brainstorming' sessions at regular intervals, both within the company's team and between other parties involved in the works. Alternatively, staff can be encouraged to meet in an informal setting, both internally as a team and with their opposite number. This could involve team members meeting within working hours or outside of work, to talk generally about the progress of the works and to raise issues that they consider possible to discuss and resolve at their level. It might well be that informal meetings will be less intimidating and more likely to bring good results if they take place in a setting other than the work site or one of the parties' offices. This must be considered by management when they make their suggestions and recommendations known to their teams.

4.9.4 Promote understanding

The intra-party and inter-party team meetings suggested above should have the effect of promoting better understanding between the team members and between the parties in general. Open forum discussions of this type will place the parties in a better position to look at their own aims and objectives in parallel with those of the other parties. They will also help the parties to understand how their respective obligations and responsibilities can blend together to provide the seamless execution of the project works that they are looking for and that the contract has been designed to encourage.

4.9.5 Discourage personal attacks

In a simple construction project context the contract is an agreement entered into by two parties: one which desires the project to be constructed and one which agrees to carry out the work necessary to meet this objective. The personnel employed by the parties to execute the works and manage the project through to completion should not take any issues relating to these works personally; they should appreciate that they have been employed for the sole purpose of executing the project works in accordance with the requirements of the contract. They must not make personal attacks on anybody, either within their own team or in another party's team. If there is an issue in contention then it has to be resolved using the mechanisms provided by the contract or, if it is an intra-company issue, by the internal procedures established by the company affected. There is no excuse that can justify a personal attack, and anyone guilty of such an action should be disciplined and/or removed from the project team. If this type of action is condoned then the other party will retaliate in a similar manner to defend its pride and self-esteem, and the dispute will escalate in a way that makes dealing with the real problem that much more difficult. If you are attacked personally, do not react emotionally. Let the other party blow off steam without taking it personally and try to understand the underlying problem behind the aggression.

4.9.6 Majority rule process

When it comes to searching for agreement on an issue, there have to be rules which the parties agree to abide by. This applies both before and during the negotiation stage. Hopefully the issue will not escalate into a full dispute, but in case it does it is good policy to decide in advance what level of agreement there has to be between the parties for a settlement to be reached.

Majority rule processes generally apply to cases where more than two parties are involved. In these circumstances it is necessary for the parties to decide among themselves whether they will adopt a majority decision or require a unanimous one.

Majority rule decisions are made by the parties casting their respective votes, with the majority decision determining the position on behalf of all parties. This can have the advantage of producing a clear-cut decision in the minimum amount of time.

The disadvantage of majority rule processes is that they do not provide incentives for the parties to compromise or to deal with issues in a way that serves the interests of all participants. Instead the majority parties only have to compromise enough to secure a decision. Once this has been achieved the interests of the other parties, those that are not part of the majority decision, can be ignored.

Rules can be built into the basic majority rule process agreement to safeguard the interests of the minority interest parties. Careful consideration should be given to listening to, discussing and adopting suggestions made by the minority parties to ensure that any settlement agreement reached takes due account of their positions and the concessions they are prepared to make to achieve a settlement. Care must be taken to ensure that the minority parties are not pressured into agreement by the unfair bargaining power of the majority parties. This may result in them having legal grounds for disputing the majority decision reached.

4.9.7 Consensus rule process

Where the parties opt for consensus rule processes the parties cannot make formal decisions on compromises and agreements unless all the parties agree. Such processes provide a basis for interest-led negotiations, and are the primary mechanism through which win–win agreements are achieved. Consensus rule processes rely to a significant extent on the parties being prepared to compromise. Consensus rule processes are likely to fail as soon as one party decides to insist on total victory, or on the absolute defeat of an opposing party.

For consensus solutions to be viable, the parties must agree upon and implement workable strategies for dealing with the many problems they will encounter along the way. The consensus building effort must therefore be framed in such a way that all parties are allowed to pursue their interests regarding the issues they are in disagreement over.

Consensus rule processes require that all parties at the table agree on all decisions that are made. There is no majority rule, and so one dissenting party can make consensus agreement impossible to attain. The parties must be able to meet and discuss the various aspects of the issues in disagreement in an open way and should hold brainstorming sessions to draw out all possible solutions. Once there is a consensus on what solutions could be adopted the parties must work together to find the one solution that all parties are prepared to support. This might be one of those put forward at the brainstorming session or one that develops through the ensuing discussions.

The advantage of consensus rule processes is that the resulting decision reached is one that meets the needs and interests of all the parties, including those with a minority interest, and is one that all parties can support, abide by and invest in. The primary disadvantage is that, depending upon the number of parties involved in the decision-making process, it can take a long time to reach a decision. Also, the chances of success are lower than with the majority rule process, which might be the best approach if a quick decision is required. If a party wants to preserve the status quo and is not in favour of change then it has the ability to stall a consensus rule process indefinitely.

When participating in a consensus rule process, parties must focus on the issues involved and inter-personal feelings must not be allowed to take control. If at the outset there is doubt as to whether a consensus can be reached on the principal issue then it would be wise to break down the issue and start the process on individual parts. The more parts that can be resolved on a consensus basis, the better the chances that eventually the whole issue in disagreement will be resolved.

If there is doubt about the parties' ability to commit fully to a consensus rule process an alternative is to introduce a mediator or facilitator into the group. This outside person could help the parties get to know each other and each other's opinions and break down any barriers preventing them from reaching a consensus.

4.9.8 Administrative decision-making process

Certain issues in contention between parties to a contract will need to be resolved by administrative decision-making processes. These processes are designed to find a balance between the conflicting interests of the parties, in much the same way as the legal system operates. Administrative decisions are generally subject to empowering legislation and will be made accordingly.

The dictionary definition of 'administrative law' is 'laws about the duties and proper running of an administrative agency that are imposed on agencies by legislatures and courts', where an 'administrative agency' is described as 'a sub-branch of the government set up to carry out the laws'.[3] Administrative law expanded greatly during the 20th century, as legislative bodies worldwide created more government agencies to regulate the increasingly complex social, economic and political spheres of human interaction.

Despite the fact that powers of administrative decision-making have generally been bestowed on the deciding bodies by legislation, such decisions are usually required in situations where none of the affected parties has a pre-defined legal right to rule on the final decision. The role of administrative law is to ensure that decisions are made fairly and with due consideration having been given to the contentions of all the parties involved.

An example of this type of decision-making process in a construction contract context would be the application of health and safety regulations. A safety issue might be in contention between the parties under the contract, but the final decision will be down to the relevant health and safety regulatory body.

Contentious issues of this nature should be referred by the parties to the appropriate regulatory body at an early stage in the discussions. To do otherwise could result in the issue escalating unnecessarily into a dispute, damaging the relationship between the parties.

4.9.9 Agreement of dispute resolution processes

Most construction contracts make provision for circumstances where the parties to the contract have encountered a dispute that cannot be resolved by mutual cooperation and discussion. This provision may well involve a form of ADR such as mediation, conciliation or adjudication prior to referring the dispute to arbitration. There will, however, be a period of time after the issue is first recognised as being contentious and it becoming necessary to resort to a formal dispute resolution procedure.

The parties should have in place an agreed process for a first attempt at resolving a contentious issue before any formal procedures need to be initiated. If this is not already addressed in the contract documents, the parties should sit down at the start of the project and agree the procedures to be followed. The parties should be in a position where lines of communication and management procedures have been agreed upon, to be brought into play once the team has exhausted all of its efforts relating to the resolution of a contentious issue. This process could involve establishing a committee comprising senior representatives of the parties who are familiar with the issue in contention. Alternatively, an independent expert in the field could be appointed to review each side's arguments and to reach a decision within a prescribed time period. The committee's or expert's decision need not be finally binding, but could have sufficient strength to empower a party to proceed with its work according to the decision and the terms of the contract, whilst still pursuing its argument under the more formal contract dispute resolution procedures.

4.9.10 Preliminary meetings

Discussions concerning a contentious issue should commence as soon as the issue becomes known. Initially, if it should be possible to resolve the issue at site level, the respective project managers should discuss it on a one-to-one basis. If the issue concerns a technical or commercial element which one or other of the project managers is not comfortable discussing, then the meetings should include technical or commercial representatives from both sides. It is important for the project managers to have with them as much information as it is possible to compile at that time in order to maximise their chances of reaching an early agreement. This should be the time when there is the greatest chance of success, particularly if the information is complete and persuasive. Preliminary meetings should continue for as long as is permissible or prescribed under the contract, or for whatever other period of time has been subsequently agreed by the parties as reasonable. If these discussions fail then the contract dispute resolution mechanisms will come into play.

4.9.11 Action-forcing mechanisms and deadlines

Where the circumstances allow, and where discussions or negotiations are not proceeding sufficiently quickly, it is a good idea to introduce mechanisms into the procedures which are designed to force actions and/or create deadlines by which decisions have to be made or actions taken. The best incentives to a contractor are payment related, whereas the best for an employer relate to savings in either time or cost. If the employer is keen to reach an agreement based on its opinion then it should obviously have a financial carrot to wave in front of the contractor, either in the form of an agreement to an additional payment if its proposal is accepted or a waiver of claims it already has against the contractor. The contractor, on the other hand, might be adamant that its opinion must take precedence, in which case the carrots to be dangled in front of the employer will generally take the form of reductions in the time for completion, savings to the contract price or a waiver of any financial or time claims it has against the employer.

Action-forcing mechanisms are of little value on their own and should have deadlines attached that set the period during which the proposals are open for acceptance. If they are not agreed within the allotted time then the other party will face the prospect of the proposals being withdrawn or amended to incorporate less favourable terms.

4.10 DISCLOSURE OF INFORMATION

4.10.1 Disclose all relevant information

As has been stressed many times throughout this book, dispute avoidance is all about communication and trust.

In order to prevent a dispute developing it will be essential for open discussions to take place as soon as the situation arises, and for them to be conducted in an atmosphere of cooperation. All available information pertinent to the potential dispute should be revealed by each party. If at a later date one party discovers that the other held back a particular piece of pertinent information then all the trust and confidence enjoyed by the parties up to that stage would be destroyed.

Where the particular piece of information is considered by the disclosing party to be confidential then that should be explained to the other party. Measures should be taken either to disclose those portions relevant to the potential dispute or to offer a detailed explanation of its contents in the atmosphere of trust that exists at that time. The relative advantages of disclosure or non-disclosure of a particular piece of confidential information must be weighed carefully against the disadvantages relating to loss of confidentiality and loss of trust.

4.10.2 Provide supporting information

When one party brings a potential dispute to the attention of another it is advisable that it provides all available supporting information at that time. This creates an immediate feeling of openness and cooperation between the parties that will bode well for future negotiations on the issues concerned.

If certain information is not available for reasons which the other party will understand and empathise with, then it should be mentioned. For example, a delay situation might have become apparent, but it is not possible to quantify either the full period of delay or the additional costs involved as the events causing the delay are ongoing. The other party will recognise that it would be unreasonable to expect full disclosure of facts not yet ascertainable. In this case it might be possible to compromise by agreeing to the submission of an interim assessment of time and costs as at the time of discussion, and agreeing on dates when updates will be provided, for instance at the end of each month for so long as the delay is current. This agreement could also include a period of time following the end of the delay event within which the final claim will be submitted.

4.10.3 Do not delay responses unnecessarily

It is important to avoid any delay in responding to requests for further information deemed by the other party as pertinent to an issue which may develop into, or which may already be, a dispute. The other party could view a delay in responding to a request for information as an attempt to hide that information. The very act of delaying its transference to the other party increases its importance to that party, and should it eventually be transferred it is then given a greater degree of consideration than it would otherwise have been given.

4.11 EXPECTATIONS OF PARTIES

4.11.1 Establish and understand the expectations of each party

Each party will approach a contract with its own particular hopes and expectations. The employer will probably be primarily concerned with obtaining a finished product built to the standard expected, within the time expected and at the cost expected when the contract was signed. The contractor will be expecting to be paid the amounts set out in the contract for the work carried out at the times set out in the contract, to be paid for all additional work subsequently required by the employer, and to have the employer's cooperation regarding access to and availability of the site sufficient to allow it to proceed with its works in accordance with the contract.

The contract should in itself make these expectations achievable. However, the ultimate success of this depends upon the attitudes of the parties to the contract and their understanding of its requirements. The party responsible for the preparation of the contract documentation will be aware of its own responsibilities, obligations and expectations. The party being awarded the contract should be similarly aware, provided it has undertaken an adequate study of the documentation during the tender and post-contract award periods.

Each party should ensure that staff who will be directly concerned with the management of the project on a day-to-day basis are provided with adequate training and instruction on the specific aspects of the contract that directly affect their roles. They should also be made aware of the broader picture, so that they can fully understand the reasons why other members of their and the other party's teams are taking a particular approach. In this way disputes will be minimised, if not totally eliminated, although the latter must be the ultimate aim of all concerned.

4.11.2 Agree on a memorandum of understanding, setting out expectations

Where the contract is somewhat complicated or the project is large and complex, it might be advisable for the parties to the contract to meet at an early stage and agree on a memorandum of understanding (MOU). The MOU will set out the basic principles of what each party hopes to achieve and what it expects of the other. This might have been included in the 'contractor's obligations' and 'employer's obligations' sections of the contract documents, but in their absence an MOU will not only give the parties reason to consider their obligations and responsibilities at an early stage but will also encourage them to ensure that all staff involved in the project are made aware of them. This will again reduce the chance of disputes arising.

The other time when an MOU will be useful is when a dispute has, unfortunately, been allowed to come to fruition and negotiations are envisaged with a view to settling it. In this case it is worthwhile entering into an MOU before negotiations commence, establishing exactly what each party hopes to achieve from the negotiations. This MOU should set out the basic reasons for the dispute, the issues in dispute and how each party would like to see the negotiations proceed. The MOU will not go so far as to include the compromises each party is prepared to make, but it should identify the areas that need to be discussed and those that require further research. It should also list the information each party requires from the other in order to enable both parties to make a sensible judgment.

In this way the negotiations should be concluded more quickly than would otherwise have been the case. Also, each party should feel less intimidated during the negotiation process, since it had prior notice of how the negotiations were likely to proceed and what ground would be covered, enabling it to come to the table better prepared than if an MOU had not been agreed. This prior knowledge should generate a greater feeling of comfort at the negotiating table, which in turn should contribute to a more amenable atmosphere for the negotiations. The end result should be an agreement that both parties find acceptable and the dispute being resolved in the minimum amount of time.

4.11.3 Work with the intention of expectations being achieved

The defining and setting down of each party's expectations in an MOU is a major step in the right direction, but it is totally meaningless if the MOU is then ignored. The expectations in the MOU must be given due consideration, whether in the avoidance or the settlement of a dispute.

Expectations can take a number of forms and may be technical, commercial or even political. The technical and commercial expectations will hopefully have been included in the contract documents, at least the more important ones should have been. It is highly unlikely that purely 'political' expectations would be included in contract documents: these are usually talked about but not put down on paper. Once the parties are working together and building working relationships they are much more likely to bring their political expectations to the fore, and these can actually play a large part in setting the scenario for the management of the whole project.

Technical expectations would revolve around the benefits to be obtained from the finished product, whether it is output from a power plant or increased traffic flow from a new traffic management system. The contractor's commercial expectations would include at least making the profit envisaged from the project. The employer's would include obtaining the finished project within the budget allocated.

Political expectations can start at a low level, such as where the site manager has political aspirations within their company. Internal politics such as this can be the most exasperating to try to overcome since the other party seldom has any real interest in them.

There are various other levels of political expectation, which can range from the client's promises to local or central government to promises made to accountants, shareholders etc. on profits to be made from the project concerned. These could have an effect on the contractor and the other team members, particularly if they are all local to one area and reputations are at stake. In such a case every effort will be made to uphold expectations for the benefit of all parties.

4.11.4 Do not put forward obstacles that hinder achievement

Knowing what a party's expectations are should encourage the other party to modify its actions in an attempt to marry those expectations with its own. If this is not possible then there should be a frank and open discussion on how the parties' expectations need to be modified in order that a viable working arrangement can be agreed. The worst approach would be for one party, knowing what the other party's expectations are, to take deliberate measures to ensure that these expectations cannot be achieved. This would without doubt generate a dispute out of an issue that could have been resolved by discussion and a certain degree of flexibility.

Such an attitude is to be deplored, and does not usually happen unless the parties have a history of confrontation or one party has cause to be aggrieved by the other, either on the particular project concerned or a previous one. If this is a personality issue then the personnel responsible should be replaced. If it is a company issue then this is more complicated, and will depend upon how strongly management has set the policies to be adopted and the expectations to be achieved. A strong manager might be able to overcome the inter-company animosity while still satisfying their manager's expectations by skilful use of diplomacy, tact and by building good relationships with their opposite number.

4.12 COMMON GROUND/COMMONALITIES

4.12.1 Mediated or facilitated negotiation process

Finding common ground and commonalities between parties is an extremely important element in the successful resolution of contentious issues. Disputes, or potential disputes, cannot be transformed unless the parties involved are bonded together with some sense of unity of purpose and commonality.

There is seldom a situation where no unity of purpose or commonality exists between the parties. This is particularly true in a construction contract since all the parties will have at least some degree of uniformity of intent. However, it often takes a mediator or facilitator, either selected from one of the parties or appointed jointly by the parties, to act independently to establish, through discussions and research, exactly what the common ground or commonalities are.

Mediators tend to focus on common interests as a starting point, possibly expanding their research as necessary to the values, beliefs, associations, roles and needs of the parties.

A facilitator will bring the parties together into a process of facilitated negotiation. Discussion and exploration of the parties' aims and objectives assists them to identify common ground and/or commonalities that they were previously unaware of.

These methods of approaching contentious issues cause a shift in the parties' relationships, away from an adversarial approach to one of seeking cooperative solutions. Finding common ground is not the same as setting the 'lowest common denominator'. On the contrary, its aim is to generate a new 'highest common denominator'. It is not about two sides meeting in the middle, but about both discovering the will to work together to achieve their common goals.

4.12.2 Identify as many points of agreement as possible

Whether the process is carried out by the parties alone, or whether mediators or facilitators are introduced, the principal objective for the parties is to discover as many points of agreement on common ground and commonalities as is possible. While this process is unlikely to lead to complete resolution of all the issues in contention, the more points of agreement that can be found the greater the intensity of the bond that the parties will eventually develop, and the less likely the issue in contention is to escalate into a dispute.

This process is about distinguishing between interests and positions. Interests are usually basic needs, whether they are commercial, technical, contractual or political, while positions tend to be about how to achieve those needs. Positions are generally mutually exclusive whereas interests tend to overlap.

4.12.3 Show parties they have more in common than originally thought

If efforts to find common ground and commonalities are successful they are likely to show the parties that they do in fact have more in common regarding the issue in contention than they previously thought, and that they may not be as far away from reaching a solution as they originally feared. With this increased sense of commonality the parties will be more amenable to reaching a compromise solution on the particular issues concerned. They will also be less likely to raise further contentious issues to the level that these have risen to. In future the sense of commonality will encourage the parties to resolve their differences of opinions by discussions at a lower and hopefully less emotionally charged level.

4.12.4 Soften resolve of adverse and hostile stereotypes

Another benefit of understanding the common ground and commonalities between the parties is that this knowledge will help to dispel any adverse and hostile preconceptions that one party has of the other. If it does not have the direct effect of changing attitudes and hardline approaches to the contentious issues, it will at least let members of the teams realise that adversarial approaches may not be the best ones given the degree of common ground that exists between the parties.

4.12.5 Help parties focus on core issues

The final benefit of identifying common ground and commonalities is that the process will have involved identification of the core issues in contention. Although this will rarely lead to immediate resolution of the issues, it will serve to clarify precisely what those issues are. The parties can then focus on the core issues during any negotiations and ignore those issues upon which they are on common ground.

4.13 TREATING FACT-FINDING PROBLEMS

4.13.1 Joint fact-finding

Fact-finding is recognised as an extremely important component of the communication process. Facts in this context are any pieces of technical, legal, contractual or commercial information related to the contract or to issues which have occurred subsequently, and which have an effect on the project and the parties to the contract. Fact-based issues can usually be resolved with absolute certainty; however, in some cases elements of uncertainty may remain. If decisions have to be made based on pieces of information which still have an element of uncertainty attached to them this does not give either party the desired level of comfort or satisfaction. The goal of joint fact-finding must therefore be to obtain as much reliable information as possible to assist the decision-makers in their efforts to reach a solution.

Joint fact-finding techniques have an important role to play in helping the parties resolve contentious issues. The parties develop and implement a joint strategy for investigating the various issues in dispute that involve questions of fact, which may concern contractual, commercial or technical issues. Frequently the issues in contention will be made up of several inferior issues, and the intention is initially to sort out those that can be resolved quickly from those that are more contentious and might take more time and effort to overcome.

The resolution of the minor issues will provide the parties with a greater depth of information, which can be used by them in the continuing discussions aimed at settling the outstanding issues.

4.13.2 Oversight committees

Where joint fact-finding efforts are considered or found by experience to be unworkable, oversight (or independent review) committees may provide an effective alternative means of determining the credibility of facts put forward by one or other of the parties involved in a contentious issue. The parties may get together and agree to hire experts in a particular field, and in whom they have a shared trust, to review as an oversight committee the factual information provided and to make a reasoned judgment based on their experience and knowledge.

The actual processes will differ from case to case, but will generally involve the oversight committee examining the facts produced to them and the methods by which they were obtained. The experts on the committee will judge whether the facts have been obtained from a reliable source, whether they have been obtained by recognised procedures and, where applicable, whether they conform to information already in the public domain. Such facts can be checked for consistency with other established facts, whether included elsewhere in the particular contract concerned, or stated in professional, technical, legal or commercial literature of good repute or recorded case law.

The downside of this method of dispute avoidance, which can also be used in negotiating an existing dispute, is that it can be expensive; also, the experts might themselves be biased in a particular way. This is not just another name for one of the recognised ADR procedures or arbitration and it does not have the controls and safeguards that are built into the formalised models. Rather, this is an ad hoc semi-informal process arrived at by agreement between the parties and is not binding in any way unless the parties decide at the outset that it is intended to be so.

I have worked on several projects where such procedures have been adopted. In these cases the parties pre-agreed that in the event of a contentious issue arising, specific engineering consultancies would be called upon to decide the issue. Tenders were obtained from several consultancies and the chosen few were put on notice that they could be called upon at any time during the project to decide an issue. Their decision would be relied upon by the parties to the extent that work would not be delayed pending a decision and that the parties would make any payments to each other related to the experts' decisions on an interim basis. The parties were free to take this dispute further at any time should they ultimately disagree with the experts' decisions. This worked well and in most cases all parties concerned accepted the experts' opinions as the final decision.

4.13.3 Credibility demonstrations

Merely carrying out fact-finding investigations and reporting the results will be of little use unless the parties have the intention of believing those results. In the absence of credible facts the parties will simply believe what they want to, and will make uninformed decisions; such decisions often fail to achieve the desired results. To avoid this problem it is essential to take steps to build a credible platform for the decision-making process.

The fact-finding must be:

- carried out in a spirit of openness and cooperation;

- clear in its intentions;

- carried out honestly; and

- be open for examination by other parties at all times.

It must be carried out by people who are suitably qualified to do so. This must be demonstrated explicitly so that all parties have the necessary level of confidence in their credibility.

There will always be a doubt in the back of a party's mind that the party responsible for the fact-finding has manipulated the results in its favour. If this doubt is not removed at an early stage by demonstrating the credibility of the people involved in the exercise the fact-finding efforts could be weakened to such a degree that the results are meaningless. This in turn will damage the decision-making process and increase the chances that the parties will eventually pursue options that will not advance their interests. Steps must be taken at an early stage to give all parties assurance that the fact-finding efforts are worthy of each party's trust, and that they will contribute significantly to the parties' abilities to make a reasoned decision based upon the information produced as a result.

4.13.4 Impact study

Depending upon the nature of the potential dispute, it may be possible to prevent it escalating by undertaking an impact study, identifying the advantages and disadvantages, merits and shortcomings of each party's position.

This is a common procedure in public authorities and government departments. The most commonly conducted impact study is probably the environmental impact assessment, which is an integral part of most planning and development processes. The assessment enables the authorities to choose between several alternative courses of action, some of which might be a greater potential cause of dispute than others. They can then make a reasoned decision with full awareness of the reaction such a decision is likely to bring about, and can plan the actions necessary to defuse the situation before it becomes intractable.

Similar processes can be useful in resolving contentious issues that arise in the day-to-day management of a construction project. The impact study and the impact statement that follows are designed to ensure that the parties are better informed, and therefore better able to reach a reasoned solution that all can buy into. The impact statements do not themselves make recommendations, they simply reduce the uncertainty involved in the decision-making processes.

4.13.5 Dealing with uncertainty

If an issue is in contention then there must inevitably be a reason why. The parties will, in their negotiations and discussions, endeavour to discover this reason and resolve the issue. There are issues, however, which will never be resolved with 100 per cent accuracy since their outcome lies in uncertainty.

Engineers can make predictions that buildings they design will withstand earthquakes up to a certain magnitude or hurricanes up to a certain wind speed based on the models available to them at the time of design, but they cannot, with certainty, predict that the buildings will withstand these forces in every situation. The models that are being used might well be the best available at the time of design, but even these models cannot predict with complete certainty the outcomes of all of the possible scenarios.

This is just an example of how uncertainty can arise in a major construction project, but not all uncertainties are as significant as this. Lesser uncertainties still have to be accounted for and there are various ways of dealing with such issues. The key approach is one of flexibility. There is no point in a client demanding that the engineer guarantees that its work will withstand a particular set of circumstances if those circumstances were not, or could not have been, anticipated at the design stage. This is particularly so in this age of climate change and environmental turmoil, where old models are having to be revised on a daily basis.

Uncertainty issues can be dealt with by the application of risk management techniques. In the above example the design risk could be managed by the application of one or more of the following risk management strategies:

- insurance, where the insurance company takes a position on how likely the insurable event is to occur and adjusts its premiums accordingly;

- risk avoidance, where for instance the engineer might consider redesigning the structure to raise it above possible flood levels or incorporating more advanced technology to cope with the increased seasonal temperature fluctuations being experienced in the location of the new building;

- risk acceptance, where the engineer guarantees the work without significant redesign;

- risk transference, where the engineer passes on the risk to a subconsultant who carried out relevant works for the engineer under a subconsultancy agreement.

4.13.6 Alternative methods for data presentation

Many disputes arise because one of the parties does not understand fully what the other party is putting forward or is confused by procedures that are unfamiliar. These situations will arise where there is a lack of good communication; when communication fails so disputes are born.

The information provided by one party to another must at all times be clear, concise and easily digestible. If there is any item that is likely to be misconstrued, misinterpreted or misunderstood, then additional explanations must be provided to ensure that each party is left in no doubt as to the intention of the party responsible for raising that item.

If written explanations are difficult or if some other form of expression would enhance them, additional drawings, cross sections, details, pie charts, histograms etc. should be provided. An overload of information is better than a dearth, provided that the information is meaningful and directed at providing additional clarification of an issue that might otherwise have ended up in dispute. It should not merely increase the thickness of the document being presented.

CHAPTER 4 SUMMARY

1. The core competencies required of a dispute management team member will be a blend of knowledge, skills and attitude.

2. Know your contract; have an awareness of the obligations and responsibilities imposed on you by the contract.

3. Contracts are a set of rules that both sides have agreed to abide by while carrying out their respective roles and which make provision for suitable and appropriate sanctions to be applied should those rules be broken.

4. If the rules imposed by the contract are both understood and applied properly then the chances of a dispute arising are reduced.

5. The contract may seem biased towards the interests of one party, but this is of no relevance. The contract has been signed by both parties and each has to make the best of it.

6. If the contract is followed to the letter and notices are served as required, the chances of a procedural dispute arising are eliminated.

7. If issues are brought to a party's attention at a sufficiently early time there is a window of opportunity for that party to propose mitigating actions.

continued. . .

8. It will be impossible to avoid all risk and you should establish what degree of risk is acceptable before entering into negotiations with the other party.

9. Prepare several scenarios that you can call into play depending upon what strategies the other parties adopt and what route the negotiations take.

10. It is legitimate to use the contract terms and conditions to apply pressure on the other party to meet its obligations and responsibilities under that contract.

11. It is illegitimate to apply pressures that cannot be supported by the contract terms and conditions.

12. Communication and cooperation are the most important weapons in the fight against the proliferation of disputes on a construction project.

13. You can have communication without cooperation, but you cannot have cooperation without communication.

14. All parties should be made to feel that their importance to the success of the project is recognised.

15. Try to resolve a potential dispute before it reaches higher management, where the flexibility to make such an agreement is not always so readily available.

16. Each party must respect the relative standing and importance of the other.

17. There is no excuse that can justify a personal attack, and anyone guilty of such an action should be disciplined and/or removed from the project team.

18. Disputes, or potential disputes, cannot be transformed unless the parties involved are bonded together with some sense of unity of purpose and commonality.

19. The process of identifying common ground and commonalities will involve identifying the core issues in contention, enabling the parties to focus on these issues and to weed out those upon which they have common ground.

Notes

1. *Cambridge International Dictionary of Idioms*, Cambridge University Press, 1998.

2. Quote from Miriam E Wilt's 'A study of teacher awareness of listening as a factor in elementary education', *Journal of Educational Research*, 43(8), April 1950, pp.626–636.

3. *Oran's Dictionary of the Law*, 3rd Edn., Thomas Delmar Learning, 1999.

Dispute management

5

5.1 DISPUTE MAPPING

5.1.1 General scope

The emergence of a contentious issue initially produces a certain level of confusion between the parties. Interactions between the parties tend to change in depth and intensity. Levels of uncertainty, unpredictability and emotion rise, and sometimes unwise and costly decisions can be made in the absence of a full understanding of all the facts. The way in which the dispute is dealt with initially has a significant influence on how costly the process will become, and so it is important to map the dispute out at the earliest opportunity. The more complicated the issue the greater the need for effective dispute mapping.

A typical dispute map will cover such issues as:

- context;
- parties;
- causes and consequences;
- relative power;
- goals and interests;
- dynamics;
- intervention.

The dispute map can be used by each party to assist it in clarifying the dispute from its own perspective and in its own handling of the negotiations, or it can be used by all parties in an effort to understand the various parties' views on the dispute. Mediators can provide dispute maps after discussing the issues in contention with the parties. This can be a useful tool for establishing a first stage in the mediation process.

The mapping process should include the resources that can be applied to limiting and resolving the issues in contention. These may include:

- Internal limiting factors – such as relationships between the parties in contention that they may wish to continue in the future.
- External limiting factors – such as the end users of the product, who might not be parties to the contention but who might benefit by one of the parties settling in a particular manner and who might be prepared to exert influence to ensure that its preferred solution is achieved.

- Neutral third parties – the contract might include some provision for the introduction of a neutral third party or parties to look into issues such as the ones in contention and to make a judgment on them, or there might be a neutral third party who could assist in settling the issues in contention.

- Techniques of dispute management – these could be the traditional ones, such as adjudication, mediation, conciliation or the introduction of dispute resolution boards.

Mapping can, if carried out in a comprehensive manner, assist the parties to make an informed judgment as to whether there is any merit in the discussions surrounding the issue in contention carrying on further, or whether the time has come to draw a line under it, at least for the time being. If the map is shared between the parties it gives them all the chance to back off and review the issues again. The better understanding of the issues that such a map should provide may in turn encourage the parties to adopt a more flexible approach to the resolution process.

5.1.2 Context of dispute

The dispute mapper will start by identifying the context of the dispute, in particular whether there is an ongoing relationship between the parties that has a bearing on the dispute and whether the dispute has been influenced by external factors not necessarily related to the particular issue in contention.

In an internal conflict within one company, the attitude of co-workers might be influenced by a corporate atmosphere of restrictive rules and regulations, or by fears of downsizing and the resultant threat to job security. A dispute might arise as a result of other unrelated contentious issues, giving rise to preconceptions and misconceptions of the other party that in turn cloud the party's judgment on a particular issue.

The conflict mapper will endeavour to discover:

- How is the dispute being expressed by each party?

- What do the parties each perceive as their respective incompatible aims and objectives?

- What are the parties each looking for as regards acceptable solutions and are they prepared to discuss compromises?

- What is the attitude of each party to the other in the daily working environment and how is the particular dispute affecting this?

- How long has the contentious issue taken to get to the dispute stage and what efforts have each party made either to defuse the situation or prevent its escalation?

5.1.3 Identifying, understanding and involving all potential disputants

It is not always easy to identify precisely who the potential disputants may be and who within each party has the power to resolve the dispute. The dispute mapper will make this one of their first tasks. The mapper will attempt to identify the extent to which the parties are involved in the dispute and the importance that each attaches to its settlement. The primary parties are those which are directly opposed to each other in relation to the issues in contention; secondary parties are those with an indirect stake in the outcome of the deliberations but which have the potential to become primary parties as the dispute progresses.

An example of a secondary party would be a subcontractor involved in a dispute between the prime contractor and the employer. The subcontractor could either stand back and let the parties resolve their own issues, or could align itself with either the prime contractor or with the employer while not being a direct adversary of either. There might, however, come a time when the issue in contention and the solutions being discussed have a direct link to its own subcontract works, in which case it could then become a primary party.

The mapper should also identify any intervening party not involved in the dispute but which, if it became involved, would have a considerable effect on the outcome. As an example take the case of a developer employer in dispute with its prime contractor over an extension of time claim. The employer's prime interest would be to gain possession of the building within budget and as close to the contract completion date as possible, in order to pass it on to the end user and start receiving rental income at the earliest opportunity. The end user might, if it became involved, be agreeable to paying acceleration costs to shorten the completion period. From its perspective, the prospect of earlier receipt of production revenues from use of the building might outweigh considerations of acceleration costs. For this reason it is sensible to involve all potential disputants in the process of dispute avoidance and, if avoidance fails, dispute settlement.

The mapper will establish whether the parties are representing themselves or whether they have appointed external consultants to do so. The mapper will identify the different styles the individual participants are adopting in their dialogue with each other, and will then be able to judge how the different styles are interacting, what effect one party's style has on the other, how each party views the other's style, and the advantages and disadvantages of each. In this way strategies can be identified which complement and use to best advantage the different styles being adopted.

5.1.4 Causes and consequences

Causes and consequences tend to be difficult to distinguish between and, as the contention develops, tend to blend one into the other. The consequence of one issue in contention might well become the cause of a subsequent issue becoming contentious. By far the greatest cause of contention is the incompatibility of goals and interests. This is greatly increased where there is a degree of misunderstanding between the parties caused, in all probability, by a lack of effective communication.

This type of causation is more likely in an international context due to a lack of understanding of the different cultures involved and the different languages being used by the parties. Even if meetings are held in English there is no guarantee that each party has the same command of the language and a slight difference in interpretation can cause a severe misunderstanding of what the other party had said or intended. Even if the parties have a good command of the English language the native English speaker will inevitably introduce nuances that are totally lost on non-native English speakers. Meetings and discussions relating to the project works, and in particular all technical, commercial and contractual discussions, should be phrased using uncomplicated English in order to minimise the chances of misunderstandings.

I recently worked on a project where English was the language of the contract and the parties to it were Bulgarian and Japanese. Each had Bulgarian translators in attention at the progress meetings held on site. The Bulgarians spoke in their language and the Japanese spoke in English, except among themselves, when they naturally spoke Japanese. Since it is not their native tongue the level of English used by the Japanese was not as high as it might have been. The meetings regularly fell into disarray as each party's Bulgarian translators argued among themselves on how to translate statements made both in Bulgarian and in English. The contract required that each party's project manager should be fluent in English, but neither party protested that this requirement was not being adhered to as neither could comply. There is no doubt that this fuelled many disputes despite the fact that a dispute avoidance measure (that project managers must be fluent in English) was laid out in the contract.

The mapper will identify the causes of the dispute, analyse what each party hopes to gain and assess what the likely consequences are in relation to the several possible outcomes of the discussions. The consequences will not be limited to those applicable to the specific project in which the contentious issue has arisen, but will include the wider consequences for the parties. It might well be that an outcome which satisfies the parties in respect of a particular project might, by its very nature, prejudice one party against becoming involved with the other in similar projects. The consequences of future dealings between the parties have therefore to be considered when mapping the dispute and preparing strategies for resolving it. Similarly, agreements relating to additional work and extensions of time need careful consideration. Whilst the solution proposed might be the optimum solution for that project, it might result in the contractor not having the resources available to start work on another project, thereby putting that project in jeopardy.

5.1.5 Understand relative powers of opposing parties

The opposing parties will inevitably be dominated by one which believes that it possesses the strongest influence over the settlement of the issues in contention. More often than not this is the employer, which believes that through holding the purse strings it can dictate how events will turn out. In some cases the contractor believes that it holds the strongest position, since the date for completion is critical to the employer and/or end user's projected cash flows.

The mapper will need to determine what dictates exist in relation to the issue in contention. They will also need to establish what each party sees as the parties' dependencies on one another, and in particular its own dependencies on the other party. The mapper will need to establish what powers each party holds, how it intends to use them and how it views the powers of the other parties. The impression that each party has of the relative powers of the others will have a significant bearing on how each party prepares its strategies and approaches the dispute. If the mapper believes that one party has more or less power than it believes it has or than it is currently utilising, they should give due consideration to this in the preparation of the dispute map.

5.1.6 Dispute dynamics

Generally speaking disputes have common, albeit not always predictable, dynamics which can be used by an intervener, whether a mediator or an independent expert, to identify a solution acceptable to all parties. Dispute dynamics can be described as the actions and reactions of the parties, and the events that these actions and reactions provoke or eliminate. The intervener's tasks will include reversing the dynamics that caused the issues to come into contention and changing them into dynamics of resolution.

The principal dynamics that will need to be considered are:

- Precipitating events – these would be the events which initiated the contention or which brought the issue in contention to the parties' attention.

- Issue emergence, transformation and proliferation – as the contention develops and discussions become more detailed, the initial issues will become more detailed; they will then be transformed as matters of principle are brought into the debate; they will then proliferate as ancillary issues are introduced into the discussions.

- Polarisation – the longer the issues remain unresolved the greater the chances of the parties polarising into groups of interested parties, and of groups and individuals polarising within each party's negotiating team. Polarisation can either be negative, leading to an increase in the intensity of the debate, or positive, leading to simplification and resolution of the contentions.

- Spiralling – spirals can be escalatory or de-escalatory. In the former the discussions intensify the disagreements between the parties, damaging the chances of finding a solution. In the latter the parties combine to reduce the number and intensity of the issues in contention and make progress towards reaching an early settlement.

- Stereotyping and mirror imaging – parties will either categorise their opposing parties according to preconceived stereotypes or they will envisage them as the mirror image of themselves. Both these attitudes will contribute to a general lack of flexibility in their approach to the issues in contention, increasing the level of miscommunication and misunderstanding between the parties.

5.1.7 Dispute intervention

Having completed the tasks outlined in the previous paragraphs of this section, the stage is now ready for intervention to be planned and implemented. The intervener will start by choosing a method by which the intervention plan can be implemented and will set a timescale for its implementation. The intervener might consider it more appropriate to apply several small planned interventions than to try to resolve all the issues at one go. The first small interventions might have the effect of bringing the parties together and introducing them to a different train of thought. This may in turn encourage the parties to apply this different approach to all issues in contention and to reach a solution among themselves.

The types of interventions traditionally available are prevention, management, settlement, resolution and transformation. A combination of these interventions could be applied if considered appropriate at the time. The intervener has to give careful consideration to which parties are to be included in each intervention, and their decision will depend upon, and be limited by, the procedures which the parties are restricted to within the contract and within their own organisations. Decisions will also need to be taken on the level at which the intervention is considered most appropriate. This will depend on the nature of the issues in dispute, the stage that the discussions have reached and the length of time that these discussions have been ongoing. It might be considered more appropriate for the initial intervention to take place at middle management level, reserving senior management level intervention for a later date should the initial intervention fail.

5.2 SELECTING THE RIGHT APPROACH TO A POTENTIAL DISPUTE

5.2.1 Direct approach

This may be the best approach, but it will depend on the nature of the potential dispute and the circumstances surrounding it. The basis of a direct approach is that a party's team leader confronts the issue head on, faces the issues as they are and views the respective stances of each of the parties objectively. Any comments made to another party in relation to the issue in contention must be constructive if this approach is to bring positive results, and criticism should be avoided. The direct approach relies on the use of problem-solving techniques and usually leaves each party with a feeling of satisfaction that a solution has been found that prevents the potential dispute escalating.

5.2.2 Bargaining

Where the parties to a potential dispute each have an idea as to how it could be resolved, other than in a win–lose scenario, they should resort to bargaining, which introduces the concept of compromise. Each party must be prepared to give way on at least some part of its demands, the difficult decision being how far such a compromise should go. It often helps if the parties each nominate one person who can lead the bargaining exercise on its behalf, possibly the team leader, project manager, commercial manager or some other equally capable person who is fully conversant with and understands the issues involved. Bargaining usually ends with each party feeling equal measures of satisfaction that a solution has been achieved and dissatisfaction that its original intentions had to be compromised to some extent.

5.2.3 Enforcement

Enforcement is an option only within one party's organisation, and is a harsh method of dealing with an 'in-house' contentious issue. This will require the team leader or responsible manager to enforce the team leader's or company's policy towards the issue concerned, and applies where the individual towards whom enforcement is directed is obviously not prepared to go along with the team decision. Unfortunately this approach can lead to resentment and, unless the individual concerned totally accepts the enforcement, it will be necessary to find a replacement team member at the earliest opportunity so that the team is not disrupted by the ensuing resentment.

5.2.4 Retreat

Retreat is practised where the issue in contention is considered not to be serious or may even only have arisen because of someone's misunderstanding of a situation. In such a case the best approach might be to retreat and simply avoid the issue for as long as is possible. In this way, particularly with minor misunderstandings, the issue might well resolve itself as the individual concerned realises their mistake or comes to terms with the fact that the issue is not really worth building up into a full-blown dispute. This approach requires good judgment and should only be used by experienced managers who have the ability to differentiate between a minor issue and one that has the potential to develop into something more significant and which needs to be dealt with accordingly.

5.2.5 De-emphasis

Where parties stand back and analyse the issues which are causing concern, and which have the potential to escalate into full-blown disputes, they often find that they do in fact agree on a number of the areas concerned. If they can reach agreement on these areas they are then able to move the discussions in a different direction. The original issues in contention are then said to have been de-emphasised, the emphasis having been transferred to the areas of agreement.

5.3 REACTIONS TO A DISPUTE

5.3.1 Agree on issues giving rise to dispute

Prior to commencement of negotiations it is wise to reach a formal agreement on the issues in dispute so that each party is totally and unequivocally aware of exactly what issues are to be the subject of the subsequent discussions. A formal document listing the issues agreed as being in dispute should be circulated among the parties as part of the MOU mentioned in earlier sections of this book. The MOU should also list the time and cost implications of each of the issues to the extent relevant.

5.3.2 Clarify issues

Disputes very often occur because of misunderstandings or failures in communication between the parties. When agreeing the MOU, a necessary pre-requisite to the commencement of formal negotiations, the narrative setting out the party's position should explain with the greatest clarity exactly how the dispute has come about, what the issues are and what the facts are, as evidenced by supporting documents. Should the other party still be unclear as to any aspect of the dispute, the issues that it is unclear about should be submitted to the other party for further clarification prior to commencement of negotiations. There is no point in commencing negotiations until both parties are completely clear on the issues involved, the other party's position as regards these issues and the evidence submitted in support of such position.

5.3.3 Attack the problem not the person

It is important that a dispute situation is dealt with in an impersonal manner. This does not mean that the parties to the dispute must ignore each other outside of the dispute negotiations; rather it means that they must approach the problem in dispute unemotionally and must disregard any personal feelings they may have concerning the other party's representatives at the negotiation. Once disputes become personal the chances of reaching an early and amicable settlement vanish.

5.3.4 Defuse the situation

Disputes are emotive subjects and the disputants can, if they are not careful, become so involved in presenting their own case that they lose all sense of reason; as a result, tempers can become frayed. Assuming that the dispute has not yet reached the stage of being presented to a mediator, adjudicator or arbitrator for resolution, and is still being discussed by the parties concerned, it should be possible to diffuse the situation by a mixture of tact, diplomacy and strategic management of the resolution process. Once it is submitted to ADR or arbitration the relevant formal rules will come into play and management of the resolution processes will be taken out of the hands of the disputants. It will then be up to the mediator, adjudicator or arbitrator to manage the parties in such a way as to minimise the occurrence of unpleasant and distracting outbursts.

5.3.5 Avoid polarisation

As disputes drag on the parties' representatives tend to become polarised in their thinking. Polarisation is the process that causes all those involved in a dispute, not only those directly involved in the negotiations, to take sides. If there is no flexibility in the approach of the negotiators and if one party refuses to understand the other party's perspective or attempts to reach a compromise then it is likely that both parties will become polarised in their respective corners. Polarisation can, if the negotiations extend over a period of time, affect not only the parties but also their advisers and associates.

A dispute between a contractor and an employer may well, if it drags on, have the effect of polarising the thoughts of a subcontractor or consultant not directly involved in the dispute but which might be affected indirectly by its outcome. It might be that it has influence over one of the parties in the dispute and could use this to the detriment of the other party, thereby ruling out the chances of them reaching a negotiated settlement.

For this reason, among many others touched on elsewhere in this book, it is essential that the dispute negotiations are entered into by all parties in a spirit of mutual cooperation and with the agreed intention of reaching a solution that satisfies everyone. It only takes one party to become so polarised in its views that it rules out all chances of the parties reaching an agreement, at which stage the whole negotiation process breaks down.

5.3.6 Examine the issues and the cases put forward impartially

All dispute negotiations should be handled impartially. Negotiations should be based upon the documentation exchanged by the parties rather than on preconceived ideas and opinions not borne out by the facts documented. In practice this can be difficult to achieve, particularly where members of a negotiating team have been involved continuously since the issues first came into contention. If partiality does come into play, the chances of reaching an agreement on the disputed issues are reduced. Therefore, every effort must be made to introduce members into the negotiating team who are relatively new to the issues being negotiated and have had less opportunity to become polarised in their views.

5.3.7 Respect before judging

We all have the same rights to hold and express our own opinions, and these opinions should be respected for what they are. The same premise should be applied when attempting to resolve disputes in a business environment. The other party's views should be given due consideration and all the evidence and statements provided by that party in support of its case should be treated with the respect they deserve before any judgment is made. It is difficult to adopt this attitude where the other party is seen not to be approaching the negotiations seriously, but even in such a situation it is necessary to treat the approach with some degree of respect.

The other party's method of approach might well have been imposed on its negotiating team or by company policy, or the individual presenting the case might believe that in adopting such an approach it is supporting the best interests of the company. The only time when it would not be appropriate to respect the other party's approach would be where it is seen to be putting forward alleged facts that are blatantly incorrect or fraudulent.

5.3.8 Concentrate on interests not positions

In a dispute situation it is very easy to forget how and where the dispute originated and what solution would ultimately be in the best interests of the parties and of the project. The negotiating teams will have commenced the negotiations by taking certain positions that they believed were in the best interests of their company. They must not get so concerned with maintaining these positions that they overlook the developing situation and how this would affect both their company and the project. The other party might not be reconsidering its own position as much as would have been liked, but it might well be proposing compromises or solutions in other areas that would prove beneficial in the longer term to the company and to the project. It is important to keep the bigger picture in mind at all times, and it is dangerous to put the initial positions before the best interests of the company and the project. It is wise to take time out at frequent intervals during the negotiations in order to take stock of where they are going and to reassess the positions that need to be taken if a mutually acceptable solution is to be reached.

5.3.9 Hold brainstorming sessions to find potential solutions

The intention of dispute negotiations must be to reach a solution that the parties can agree on as resolving the issues in contention to their mutual satisfaction. With this in mind all avenues must be explored in order to achieve this goal. Inter-party and intra-party brainstorming sessions are an ideal way of spreading the debate among all those involved and drawing upon the opinions of the different members of the teams. These opinions may be of no relevance, may be against company policy or may simply not be worth pursuing, but the exercise may well prove to be worthwhile by bringing out a few opinions and suggestions that could prove beneficial in the search for an acceptable solution. There is nothing to lose and everything to gain in holding brainstorming sessions and, should the dispute remain unresolved at the end of the negotiating process, the parties will at least feel that they have given it their best shot.

5.3.10 Summarise issues

At the end of each round of negotiations a summary should be prepared confirming any agreements reached and any changes to the issues in contention. Each party will then be clear as to where it stands before taking the next step in the resolution process.

5.4 CONTROL TECHNIQUES

5.4.1 Assertiveness

Assertiveness is a style of behaviour that allows an individual to express their feelings in an honest, clear and respectful way that does not insult people. It enables you to stand up for your rights while knowing that what you say is not necessarily the only valid truth. Although this style of behaviour is beneficial most of the time it does not mean that you will always get what you want. The results of being assertive are that you feel good about yourself, and that other people know that there is nothing vague about dealing with you. Being assertive means being prepared for confrontation, and it takes courage. Some people find it harder than others because of their natural easy-going style and therefore more practice is required before they are able to use this skill to their full advantage. The aim should not be just to gain a win, it should be to solve the problem and obtain the best result for the party and for the project.

Assertiveness involves the following:

- Being confident about handling yourself in a dispute situation.

- Being clear about what you want and how it can be achieved.

- Keeping calm and sticking to the point.

- Being able to communicate without attacking the other party.

- Saying 'yes' when you want to and 'no' when you mean 'no'; rather than agreeing with others in either your own or the other party's team just to please someone else.

- Deciding on, and sticking to, clearly defined boundaries, and being happy to defend your position.

- Being able to listen to others.

- Having confident, open body language.

- Having a positive, optimistic outlook.

- Being honest with yourself about your feelings.

- Repeating your message after listening to the other party's point of view, even if you meet objections.

- Trying to propose alternative solutions.

- Pointing out calmly when the other party tries to create a diversion and repeating your message.

- Always respecting the rights and points of view of the other party.

When someone does not know how to express themselves assertively, they tend to resort to either aggression or to more passive modes of communication in an attempt to punish or undermine the other person. They may play games, use sarcasm, give in resentfully or remain silent, at their own cost.

One of the myths about assertive behaviour is that it involves being aggressive. This is not true. Assertiveness involves clear, calm thinking and respectful negotiation within a space where each person is entitled to their own opinion. Aggression involves bottling up feelings that eventually explode, leaving no room for communication.

Other people may think that being assertive is about being selfish; it is in fact the opposite. Assertiveness is about acknowledging all opinions as important. An assertive attitude says 'I matter and you do too'. Learning how to express yourself assertively can seem daunting at first, but there are many things you can do to help you become more assertive.

5.4.2 Questioning skills

One of the stock phrases used when discussing computer applications is 'garbage in, garbage out', meaning that if you put the wrong information in then you will get the wrong information out. The same principle applies to communication: if you ask the wrong questions, or frame them in the wrong way, you will get the wrong answers back, or at least not the answers you were looking for.

Asking the right question is one of the first principles of effective communication. By asking the right questions at the right time you can obtain better information, encourage others to give more thought to the issues concerned, learn more about the other party, build stronger relationships and manage people more effectively.

There are various types of questions, each of which elicits a different type of response:

- Open questions – these usually begin with such words as 'what', 'why' and 'how'. Open questions are good for finding out more detail and another party's opinions on specific issues.

- Closed questions – these usually only require a very short answer, either 'yes', 'no' or a specific piece of information such as a name or address. They do not expect the answer to be expanded on in any way. These are good for testing knowledge, concluding a discussion or making a decision.

- Funnel questions – this questioning technique starts with asking a general question and then homing in on each point in the answer, asking more and more detailed questions as the answer trail develops. Funnel questions are good for delving deeper into detail about a specific issue, sequences of events etc.

- Probing questions – this is another strategy used to find out more detail about a specific issue. Information already established in the response to a previous question is used to dig down a little further. Probing questions are good for gaining clarification of an issue and for drawing information out of a party who is reluctant to tell you the whole story.

- Leading questions – these try to lead the respondent to your way of thinking, either by stating an assumption, by ending with a personal appeal such as 'wouldn't you agree?', by phrasing the question so that the easiest response would be 'yes', or by giving the other party two choices of response, both of which you would be happy with. Leading questions are good for getting the answer you were hoping for while leaving the other party feeling that it actually had a choice, and for closing a negotiation.

- Rhetorical questions – these are not really questions but are statements phrased in a questioning format that do not really expect an answer. They are good for engaging the other party.

Questions are a good way of avoiding misunderstandings, expanding knowledge, diffusing a heated situation and encouraging the other party to embrace your opinions.

5.4.3 Handling difficult situations

Difficult situations can take up a great deal of time and energy, especially when we do not accurately focus on the problems themselves. Most of us tend to focus on who is involved rather than on what is occurring, whereas we should be focusing on the issue in contention.

The four most crucial steps in handling difficult situations are:

- Step 1 – Identify the real issue (difficult situation).
- Step 2 – Clarify your role to see if, or how, you can influence the difficulty.
- Step 3 – Evaluate the alternatives that might help resolve the difficulty.
- Step 4 – Discuss the difficulty and the alternatives with the parties involved.

Step 1 – Identify the real issue

Identifying the real problem is the most complex of these steps. Often it is not difficult to find out what happened; the real challenge is to work out how to fix what happened.

Put aside emotions and identify which problems are, in reality, relatively minor and will eventually resolve themselves. As you filter out these elements, you will find you are left with one issue that absolutely demands your attention.

To proceed positively through a situation, you must first agree that the problem has been correctly identified. Then focus on what you can do now and, instead of talking about each difficulty, begin to identify those areas you can change. When you focus on issues instead of individuals you avoid unproductive fault-finding and other similarly secondary symptoms.

Step 2 – Clarify your role

After identifying the real issue, clarify those facets of the difficulty that are within your ability to change. Being clear about possible action gives you the opportunity to determine who is in the best position to act. If you neglect to clarify your own role in achieving resolution, the difficulty may continue, or even escalate. If you say nothing, you are indicating that nothing can be done about the situation. Clarifying roles makes sense. You direct your energy where you have the greatest chance of achieving a successful outcome.

Step 3 – Evaluate the alternatives

It is critical to evaluate the alternatives and their possible impacts carefully because you need to align your efforts with business objectives. Alignment can be accomplished only after the real issue has been correctly identified and your role clearly defined. Evaluating alternatives also involves thinking creatively, calculating risks and considering new ways to look at old challenges.

Step 4 – Discuss the difficulty

To align effort and goals it is essential that you discuss the real issue and the alternative you have selected for handling it. Interestingly enough, this fourth step, which is basically discussion, is the easiest in the process, yet it is also the most often neglected. We sometimes forget the importance of keeping others informed and involved. Discussing the difficulty with everyone involved offers multiple benefits: it ensures buy-in, answers questions and provides an opportunity to evaluate how the chosen alternative will affect everyone concerned. Once you learn how to handle a difficult situation it is no longer as confusing or frustrating.

Conclusion

We cannot make difficulties go away. Yet what we think of as a difficulty may in fact be an opportunity. Using this four-step process allows us to discern the underlying causes of a particular event or problem. In turn, that knowledge may stimulate our thinking, motivate us to greater accomplishments and challenge us in new ways. The better we learn to anticipate difficulties and thereby lessen their frequency and impact, the better we can focus on the best use of our time, energy and resources.

5.4.4 Escalation prevention

In order that you can prevent escalation of a potential or current dispute you must be constantly aware of the state of any negotiations and discussions. You must be able to recognise any changes in the attitudes of the parties taking part in the negotiations that might result in escalation.

It is important that you are able to recognise a potential escalation of a dispute and appreciate the measures that can be taken to prevent this from occurring. It might be that simply spending more time listening to the other party's point of view will allow you to reason with it and eliminate any threat of escalation by making proposals or taking actions that satisfy the party's concerns, at least for the time being.

A simple apology for a situation that has been misinterpreted by the other party is another escalation prevention tool. However, this also requires an understanding of the situation that can only come from being attentive to all negotiations and having the ability to read the signals being given off by the other party.

Often when a party expresses its opinion in anger there is a small percentage of truth in what they are saying. If you accept this element of truth and make this known to the other party, you instantly take away an element of the resistance that was there previously. This serves to dampen down emotions and prevent further escalation of the dispute on those particular grounds.

5.4.5 Mirror imaging

Mirror imaging is a strategy that used to make the parties assess the reasonableness of their behaviour. Each party is asked to look at itself the way others see it, and to make appropriate changes if it does not totally agree with or like what it sees. Often if a party to a dispute looks at itself honestly it will notice that it is doing the same kind of things that it faults the other party for doing. Once this is understood the party can change its behaviour to appear more reasonable, without altering or undermining its true interests, and the escalation of the dispute will be prevented.

5.4.6 Resolve issues at an early stage

It is imperative that all contentious issues are resolved at the earliest opportunity. If they are allowed to drag on and fester then the chances of their resolution are diminished. If contentious issues are addressed immediately – while the parties have the representatives concerned available to enter into discussions and offer explanations of the issues concerned – there is a far greater chance that a mutually acceptable solution will be reached. If the issues are left until the end of the project, many of the project staff will have been demobilised and transferred to other projects. It is easy to understand how an issue fresh in everybody's mind is simpler to resolve than one that occurred several years previously.

5.4.7 Accept rather than challenge

Not all issues that could be contentious end up in dispute. Sometimes it is more sensible for a party to make a judgment that an issue is not of sufficient importance, or does not have sufficient impact, to justify the costs of confrontation. In such circumstances it would be better to resolve the issue by accepting, rather than challenging, the situation and simply 'agreeing to disagree', or by accepting the situation as a disagreeable but unavoidable fact of life.

5.4.8 Find common ground

Wherever possible parties to a potential dispute should try and find some common ground between. This will help them develop an agreement that goes at least part way to resolving the issues in contention. It is rare to find a potential dispute where the parties do not have some common ground, and once this has been identified the parties should be able to reach agreement on those issues to which the common ground relates. With those parts no longer being contested the parties then have a significantly greater chance of resolving the remaining issues without them progressing into disputes.

5.4.9 Transform a dispute by directing it

The parties to a dispute have the power to transform the dispute through their own actions. If they adopt some of the control techniques outlined above they will be in a stronger position to direct the way in which the dispute progresses. The dominant party will be the party who has taken active control of the dispute negotiations. The passive party will have less chance of attaining its goals than will the active party.

5.5 ANALYTICAL PROBLEM SOLVING

5.5.1 Identify fundamental sources of dispute

The analytical problem-solving approach is particularly suited to large construction projects, where the issues in contention can be multi-faceted and linked with a series of events and issues far beyond their immediate area of operation. It is an approach that is recommended if:

- you are continuously 'firefighting' and 'solving' the same problems without getting to the root cause;
- you want a fast, efficient and standardised approach to results-focused root cause determination and resolution;
- you want to get in front of problems and prevent them from occurring;
- your company seems to swing between crazy, off-the-wall ideas which are not really practicable and the 'same old thing'.

The combination of analytical techniques with creative talent will enable you to:

- pinpoint root causes using facts, not guesswork or opinion;
- avoid costly trial and error by testing solutions before their implementation;
- identify and target potential problems before they happen and develop plans to prevent them.

The first aim of analytical problem solving is to locate the source of the potential dispute and then isolate the factors that affect it and that it in turn affects. Once these have been isolated it will be possible to decide on which analytical strategy is best suited to the issues. Some approaches are more theoretical, such as brainstorming, whereas others are more specific, such as critical path analysis.

In carrying out the analysis it is often best to involve personnel who are not directly concerned with negotiations. They will be more likely to suggest new approaches that those more deeply involved in the issues might not consider. The formal negotiators can then consider whether to approve and implement the strategies proposed. The various forms of analytical problem solving most often used on construction projects will now be discussed in more detail.

5.5.2 Brainstorming

Brainstorming, mentioned briefly earlier, involves developing creative solutions to problems. It works by focusing on a contentious issue and coming up with as many solutions as possible. Initially there is no restriction on the feasibility or viability of the solutions proposed; the aim is to sow the seeds for more serious solutions as the session continues.

The team leader or manager in charge of the brainstorming session should take control of the session and define the issue to be resolved, specifying any criteria that must be accounted for. They will steer the session but should at the same time encourage an enthusiastic, uncritical attitude among the brainstorming team. There should be a defined timescale for the initial session and the leader should steer it towards the development of practical solutions.

The participants should be drawn from all sections of the project team and, depending upon the nature of the issues in discussion, should not necessarily be restricted to management. If the issues in contention are technical then there is ample justification to include technicians and engineers so that their input can be considered alongside that of management. The same criteria should be applied whatever the nature of the dispute.

The whole session should be kept as light-hearted as possible, even though the result will hopefully be the identification of some serious proposals for resolving the issues being discussed. At this stage criticism of ideas should be avoided, as should serious evaluation. If criticism in particular was encouraged it would have the effect of stifling free and original thought, the very thing the brainstorming session is trying to encourage.

5.5.3 Decision trees analysis

Decision trees are excellent tools for making financial or number-based decisions where a lot of complex information needs to be taken into account. They provide an effective structure in which alternative decisions and the implications of taking those decisions can be laid down and evaluated. They also help the parties form an accurate, balanced picture of the risks and rewards that can result from a particular choice.

To start with, a situation has to occur where a decision has to be made. As indicated in Figure 7, draw a box towards the left hand edge of a large piece of paper, and from this box draw lines extending towards the right-hand edge, one line for each possible solution that you are aware of. Write the solution along the top of the relevant line. The lines should be well spaced out, enabling expansion of the solutions as discussions develop.

Fig. 7 Decision Tree Analysis

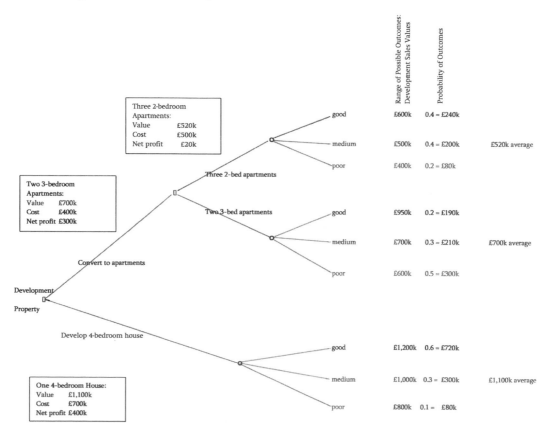

Draw a circle at the end of each solution line representing the result. However, if a further decision has to be made then draw a small square at the end of the line – squares represent decisions and circles represent uncertainty or random factors. If you have completed the solution at the end of the line then leave it blank.

Starting from the new decision squares on the diagram, draw out lines that represent the options available. From the circles on the diagram draw out lines representing possible outcomes, again noting on the line what it represents. Carry on doing this until you have drawn down as many of the possible outcomes and decisions as you can see leading on from your original decision box.

Review the tree diagram that you have now drawn and challenge each square and each circle to see if there are any solutions or outcomes you have not considered. If there are, draw them in, redrafting the tree as necessary to avoid congestion.

Evaluation of the decision tree can now commence, the aim being to calculate which decision has the greatest worth to you. Start by assigning a cash or numeric value to each possible outcome, identifying how much you consider it to be worth to you.

Next examine the points of uncertainty (circles) and estimate the probability of each outcome. If you base this assessment on percentages then the total of each circle must add up to 100 per cent (fractions must add up to 1). These estimates should be based upon data relating to past events, where this is available, otherwise they should be your best educated guess based on the knowledge and information available to you.

To calculate tree values, multiply the value of each outcome by its probability. This will give you the value of that option. Then deduct the cost of that option (which you will have estimated separately) from the value, which will give you the benefit of that decision. When you have calculated the benefit of each decision you are then in a position to select the decision that has the greatest benefit to you and adopt that as your chosen decision.

In the example provided in Figure 7 it can be seen that at the beginning of the exercise there was uncertainty as to whether to develop a site by building three two-bedroom apartments, two three-bedroom apartments or one four-bedroom detached house. By working through the analysis it can be seen that, based on the probabilities which were deemed appropriate to use from past experience of similar developments in the area, the most viable option would be to build a four-bedroom detached house.

Decision trees provide an effective means of decision-making because they:

* clearly lay out the problem so that all choices can be viewed, discussed and challenged;

* provide a framework to quantify the values of outcomes and the probabilities of achieving them;

- assist us in making the best decisions on the basis of the existing information and our best guesses.

Decision trees are invaluable tools for the internal assessment of options available when there is a potential dispute with another party. It enables each party to decide which approach would be the best one for it and also identifies the extent to which the alternative choices, some of which will have been proposed by the other party, would be to its disadvantage should they be adopted. As with all decision-making methodologies, decision trees should be used in conjunction with a degree of common sense.

5.5.4 Force field analysis

This method of analysis looks at the various forces acting for and against a particular course of action, so that a decision can ultimately be made which takes account of all interests. If this is being carried out retrospectively, where a decision has already been made, a force field analysis will help you identify the forces acting for and against the decision, and help you plan to reduce the impact of the opposing forces and reinforce the supporting forces.

To start with, list all the forces acting for a particular course of action in one column and all the forces acting against it in another column. Assign a score to each force on the basis that 1 is weak and 5 is strong. A simple example of a potential in-house dispute is shown in Figure 8, where a construction company is trying to decide whether it should or should not outsource its design office workload to consultants.

Fig. 8   Force Field Analysis

Issue: Whether to Outsource Design Office Work			
Forces for Decision	Score	Forces against Decision	Score
Reduction in overheads increases company's long-term viability	5	Loss of in-house staff, creation of unrest among remaining workforce	4
Increase in overall efficiency of project work	4	Lack of continuity of workforce	3
Increase in flexibility of staff usage	4	Learning curve each time new design engineers involved	3
Ability to cope with variances in workloads	4	Less opportunity for feedback to in-house staff for the ultimate benefit of future projects	4
Release of management time enabling them to deal with other issues	3	Lack of management control	2
Total Score	20	Total Score	16

Once the analysis has been completed the viability of the change can be determined. In this example measures can be taken to eliminate the fears of the existing staff and to encourage them to adopt the proposed course of action by showing them the benefits to the company of proceeding with the changes and that without the proposed action the company is likely to be less competitive, thereby putting their jobs at risk. It is always better to reduce the strengths of the forces opposing change than to increase the strength of those pushing the proposal forward.

5.5.5 PMI (Plus, Minus and Interesting)

This is a simple device which can be used where there is a number of alternative solutions to a contentious issue. For each option simply draw a table with three columns marked 'plus', 'minus' and 'interesting', as shown in Figure 9. In the plus column list the positives to be gained by implementing that option. In the minus column list all the negative effects and in the interesting column list all the extended implications of implementing the option, whether these implications are positive or negative.

Attribute subjective scores on a 1 to 10 scale to each point in the plus and minus columns, taking account of the influence of the interesting column. The total score of each of the plus and minus columns should then suggest whether the proposed option should be taken forward, a high plus score indicating that the option should be favoured and a high minus score indicating that the option should be avoided. This is not a highly scientific method of analysis but can be a useful tool under certain circumstances.

5.5.6 SWOT analysis

SWOT stands for Strengths, Weaknesses, Opportunities and Threats. A SWOT analysis is performed by writing down answers to the following questions in relation to each possible solution to a potential dispute:

- the advantages of pursuing each option;
- the disadvantages of pursuing each option;
- the opportunities to be gained by pursuing each option;
- the obstacles to be faced in pursuing each option.

In a potential dispute situation involving several parties it is useful for each party to complete a SWOT analysis for each of the options they have agreed are available to them. They may well find that they actually agree on more points than they initially thought they did, and this can be a positive aid in reaching an acceptable solution without entering into a dispute scenario.

Fig. 9 PMI Analysis

Issue in Contention: Whether or not contractor would benefit by accelerating works which have been delayed due to late deliveries		
Plus	Minus	Interesting
Contract completion date could be achieved, giving good impression of contractor's ability Score of 8		Employer may not be in urgent need of premises and may prefer to waive liquidated damages for delay rather than pay acceleration costs
	Uncertainty of ability to recover additional costs from employer Score of 8	Acceleration claim would have to be prepared to enable additional costs to be recovered, involving further expense of specialist consultants and further uncertainty
	Availability of additional resources not yet confirmed Score of 4	Quiet time in local construction market, no labour problem, but material shortages may still be a problem
Risk of liquidated damages would be eliminated Score of 6		Possibly more viable to pay liquidated damages than to pay additional costs of acceleration
	Acceleration might still not be sufficient to achieve contract completion date and eliminate liquidated damages totally Score of 3	Contractor would at least have showed it was trying to mitigate delays and liquidated damages would be less than would otherwise be the case
Project team could be diverted to next project sooner Score of 3		No firm date for commencement of next project yet agreed
Employer satisfaction could influence future projects our way Score of 0		Employer is not planning any future work; current project may be a 'one off' project
Total Plus Score = 17	Total Minus Score = 15	
Scores indicate that acceleration is the best option		

5.6 FRAMING

5.6.1 Definition

Frames are interpretive lenses through which individuals view and make sense of unfolding events. Framing in the context of dispute avoidance means the process of describing, interpreting and understanding an event, focusing attention on what the potential dispute is all about and what should be done about it. Different frames can be held by different parties. Each party to a dispute has its own perceptions as to why the dispute arose, the relevance of factors leading up to the dispute, their priorities, the alternative solutions and the risks associated with each alternative solution.

Framing techniques are used to clarify why a dispute exists and identify what actions are critical to it, why the parties act as they do and how they should respond. Frames can, however, have the effect of perpetuating intractable disputes and tend to limit the clarity with which a party views the dispute, and they can even contribute to the escalation of disputes.

Changes in the context of the dispute or intentional interventions can have the effect of reframing the dispute and increasing its tractability, and the introduction of reframing can be a particularly effective strategy during the management of disputes. Reframing is the term used to describe the purposive management of frames and has the following goals:

- To clarify or refresh the perception of the issues in dispute in order to promote more productive information exchange.

- To stimulate new ideas, to expand the framework of discussion and to explore actions and solutions not previously considered.

- To sharpen the parties' understanding of their interests and how the modes of action they have chosen serve those interests in order to examine potential processes for managing conflict more productively, and to reconsider patterns of relationships between the parties.

- To identify those subjects on which the parties hold different views (even when the basis for the divergent frames is more fully understood) in order to identify opportunities for trade-offs based on clearly understood differences.

- To identify differences that cannot be bridged in order to appreciate more fully the conflict dynamics and to evaluate the potential for conflict reduction processes that do not violate these intractable differences, and also to determine the degree of importance attributed to these intractable differences and to seek ways to address them.

Thus reframing may pave the way for resolving, or at least managing, a dispute.

5.6.2 Framing focuses attention

The way in which we focus our attention on an issue depends on many factors other than simply considering what has actually happened. It is influenced in no small way by past experiences and accumulated knowledge of similar issues. Disputant parties often have preconceived ideas about each other and about themselves that influence how they view the issues in contention. These preconceptions form the basis for each party's frame, and can have negative influences on the chances of the parties reaching agreement. One party may have the impression that the other has more power, or might have had a bad experience with the other party on a different project; these factors will affect the way in which it frames the current dispute.

5.6.3 Framing determines whether a situation is seen as a dispute

A frame determines whether an issue is in fact a contentious one, and also what action, if any, needs to be taken. In a simple example, party A might object to a remark made by party B and would immediately frame the situation as a dispute, whereas party C might have taken it as a light-hearted off-the-cuff remark and ignored it. By reframing and taking account of party C's reaction to the remark, party A may well agree that it is in no one's interests to continue framing this issue as a dispute.

5.6.4 Framing determines how to deal with a situation

A frame might show that an issue previously regarded as contentious is in fact relatively unimportant, in which case a decision might be taken to ignore it. If, on the other hand, the frame shows the issue to be important, the people involved will have to decide how to deal with it. The frame might show the issue as resolvable by informal discussion or negotiation, in which case negotiations with the other party will commence. If the frame shows the dispute as more severe and less resolvable, the parties will need to instigate whatever procedures are set out in the contract for the resolution of such disputes.

5.6.5 Interest-based framing

Interest-based framing describes contention in terms of interests rather than positions. Often interests are compatible even when positions are not. Thus interest-based framing enables the parties to identify win–win solutions to problems that might not have been evident when the issues were described in terms of the parties' positions alone.

Rather than describe a contentious issue in terms of positions ('I want one thing but he wants something else', or 'we both want something that only one of us can have'), it is often helpful to reframe the contention in terms of interests. Interests are the underlying reasons why parties hold the positions they do. Making an effort to reframe a contentious issue in terms of underlying interests often makes some aspects of the issue simpler to resolve. It can reveal areas of commonality, leading to improved cooperation and relationships between the parties, and in turn settlement of the remaining issues in contention.

5.6.6 Fairness-based framing

In fairness-based framing the parties approach the contentious issue in a way that they hope will enable them to obtain what they believe is rightfully theirs. The parties define the issue in terms of justice, fairness and rights. This exercise forces them to consider what in fact is fair and how fairness or justice is determined. Fairness is not simply 'what is good for me under the present circumstances'.

Definitions of justice vary widely, especially between different nationalities and cultures. However, everybody has some standard principles by which justice is measured. In a construction dispute this will be defined, at least in part, in the conditions of contract and by the substantive laws applicable to the contract. If the situation in dispute is not covered by the contract or legislation then there will be industry standards, norms and traditions that can be used to define what in fact is fair and reasonable under such particular circumstances.

5.6.7 Needs-based framing

In needs-based framing reaction to a contentious issue is framed as being a collective effort to fulfil the fundamental needs of all parties. By eliminating the tensions which arise when one or more party's needs go unmet, this approach can sharply reduce the level of conflict.

The key to reframing based on needs is being able and prepared to identify those needs in the first place. This requires careful analysis of the dispute and of why the parties are taking the positions they are. Unlike interests, which may be structured in a win–lose manner, needs are often mutually reinforcing. The more one party gains, the more secure it feels, and the less inclined it will be to continue in contention with the other party, which in turn makes the other party feel more secure. Thus integrative (win–win) solutions are often more likely to arise in a needs-based situation than in a high stakes, win–lose, interest-based situation.

5.6.8 Integrative (win–win) reframing

When contentious issues are being approached as unavoidably win–lose situations it is often useful to ask whether it is possible to redefine the situation so that integrative (win–win) solutions can be obtained. This is especially important when the problem definition leaves no acceptable alternatives for the opponent. Although total integrative reframing is not always possible it is often possible to reframe at least part of the contention in this way.

Parties which consider an issue as a win–lose situation assume that anything it wins will cause the other party to lose, and vice versa. Integrative reframing involves focusing on the parties' interests or needs and redefining the dispute as a win–win situation. This can be achieved by expanding the resources from which the parties are drawing or redefining what the parties want out of the dispute so that each party can gain satisfaction even from limited resources.

5.6.9 Joint/assisted reframing

When opponents each frame a contentious issue in very different terms, cooperative problem-solving can be very difficult. An exercise in joint reframing can help each party see the issue in contention as the other party sees it, which can help both parties confront the situation in a more constructive manner. It can even be helpful for a party to seek a third party's assessment as to whether its view is reasonable, fair and accurate.

If a dispute ends up in front of a mediator, one of the first things a mediator will do is ask each party to explain how it perceives the problem. This allows each party to see how the other party frames the dispute. When there is a big difference in the parties' views about what the key issues of the dispute are the mediator will often try to get the parties to redefine the nature of the dispute together (assisted reframing). If the parties can work together to develop a new definition of the problem it is usually much easier for them to then work together to develop a mutually acceptable solution to the dispute, or at least to those parts of it which, as a result of reframing, are now considered resolvable.

This process of joint reframing can either take place quickly or can develop over a period of time. Parties often need time to understand the full depth of the dispute and their understanding will improve as they discuss and negotiate a solution. It can be seen from this that joint reframing is generally more effective after the dispute has been left to run for a period of time and has become 'ripe' for reframing.

In most situations the assistance of a mediator in reframing situations has significant benefits as the parties will often have a natural reluctance to engage in reframing on their own. One of the mediator's functions in such a situation would be to restate the parties' frame perceptions in a way that causes less resistance and hostility, thereby setting the scene for reaching an amicable settlement.

5.7 NEGOTIATION

5.7.1 Definition

Negotiation is best described as an interactive process between two or more parties, undertaken in an attempt to reach agreement through discussion which takes place at one or more meetings on an issue or issues of mutual interest to the parties and upon which there is currently disagreement, confusion or similar. Negotiation in the context of this book can also refer to circumstances where the parties are endeavouring to establish formal relationships with each other or to establish courses of action to be pursued.

Negotiation involves:

- the process, which includes the actual methods of negotiation, the context of the negotiations, the parties to the negotiation, the tactics used by the parties and the way in which the parties communicate; and

- the substance, which includes the subject matter of the negotiations, the agenda for the negotiations, the issues to be discussed, the possible outcomes of the negotiations and the end agreements reached.

5.7.2 Negotiation skills

Negotiation skills are among the most significant determinants of success in the resolution of contentious issues and disputes. However, few people possess these skills to the level that is necessary for them to undertake with confidence the negotiation of complex construction issues. Negotiation is something that we all do in both our personal and business lives, although this might not be immediately apparent to everyone. When we discuss what to do and where to go after work on a Friday night we are in effect negotiating with our partners and friends, the end result of which is either a compromise that suits us all or a quiet night at home in front of the TV. Communication is always the means by which negotiations are carried out, whether face-to-face, on the telephone or in writing.

The single most important factor that will enhance your negotiation skills is planning. Without proper and full preparation of your presentation the negotiations will seldom go the way you would like them to. You must have confidence in your ability to negotiate your way to success and must be sure that you can keep control of the negotiations at all times.

The parties executing the negotiations should be at similar levels within their respective organisations; it is not a good idea to have the managing director of one party negotiate with a clerk from the other. This is a definite overkill/undersell; the first party would not have the opportunity to bring in more senior management should the initial negotiations fail, and the second party would be giving the impression that it does not consider the issue serious enough to warrant the appointment of a senior manager to represent it at the negotiations.

Negotiation skills can be taught, but not everyone has the right temperament for dealing with opposing forces who might be far more experienced in and familiar with negotiation techniques. There are many different techniques used in the negotiation process. Each party will need to decide which technique to use in each particular situation, based upon the nature of the issue to be negotiated and the perceived attitude of the opposing party. If it gets it wrong there is no problem in changing the negotiator at any time during the negotiations; it is far better to change negotiator if this will provide a more effective means of achieving the desired end result. Some negotiations call for an aggressive negotiator, whereas others would be better served by a negotiator who was calmer and more prepared to spend time understanding the other party's position.

Negotiations may have to be carried out by, or the negotiating team may have to include, a particular person, possibly because of their special knowledge of the project or of a particular technical issue. If that person is not an experienced negotiator, then training will be necessary. This will need to cover not only basic negotiation skills but also general attitudes and appearances. Body language, for instance, accounts for over 90 per cent of communication and plays an important part in all negotiations, no matter what the subject matter is.

Your body language gives others a general impression of who you are, where you are coming from and what your intentions are. You can give a positive impression in a negative situation and a negative impression in a positive situation, depending upon which impression will serve you best, purely by the way in which you stand or sit, by your hand-to-face movements and by other gestures.

Those who stand always look more powerful than those who sit. Take advantage of this and if at all possible give your presentation from a standing position. If standing is not an option then you will have to make the most of your seated position. The reason why standing gives an impression of power is largely due to the space that you occupy. This principle can be applied when in a seated position by stretching your legs out or by having your arms at the side of your chair. Even when you are negotiating over the telephone and you need to be assertive, standing up to talk will project your urgency and authority despite the fact that you are not visible to the other party.

Hand-to-face movements are equally important. If the person you are addressing is holding their chin or scratching their face this could mean that they are giving serious consideration to what you are saying and that is the time to try and close the negotiation. A lot of us move our heads when we are trying to gain approval from others of what we are saying. If you want to look powerful you should keep your head movements to a minimum. Touching your nose could mean that you are not being entirely truthful in what you are saying. Similarly, folding your arms could mean that you are trying to defend yourself and will give the other party the impression that you are not overly confident in what you are saying. When you sit with arms folded, legs crossed and the body turned away slightly this gives the impression you are uninterested. If you then change your stance by unfolding your arms and uncrossing your legs this indicates that you may well be starting to accept the other party's opinion and that this is their opportunity to conclude the negotiation in their favour.

Making direct eye contact with the other party shows that you are honest and confident in what you are saying. Conversely, minimal eye contact shows that you are shy, nervous, telling an untruth or just do not like the other party. It can also mean that you think you are superior to the other party and do not need to make eye contact. A smile can put the other party at ease, whereas a frown will give the impression that you are angry, and staring continuously will give the impression of aggression.

Use body language skills in a negotiation context to make you appear more confident, powerful, trustworthy etc., depending upon the particular situation you are in and the impression you want to make. Try and read the other party's body language and, if necessary, adapt your presentation to suit.

Some negotiation techniques that can be used to good effect are:

- Look for the difference – look for items that may be more important to one party than the other; these can be traded off one against the other.

- Broaden the pie – create additional resources so that both parties can obtain their major goals.

- Non-specific compensation – one party gets what it wants and the other is compensated on another issue not necessarily part of the current negotiations.

- Logrolling – each party makes concessions on low-priority issues in exchange for concessions on issues that it values more highly.

- Cost cutting – one party gets what it wants, but the costs to the other party are reduced or eliminated.

- Bridging – neither party gets its initial demands, but a new option that satisfies the major interests of both parties is developed and agreed.

5.7.3 Preparing for a negotiation

One of the most important considerations when entering into a negotiation is to ensure that you have prepared your case thoroughly. If the issue is not a major one then excessive preparation might be counterproductive because of the length of time spent on it, time that could have been better spent on other matters. If the negotiation relates to a major issue then the importance of serious preparation cannot be overemphasised. Consider the following questions before commencing your negotiation:

- Your goal – what do you want to gain from the negotiations? What does the other party want?

- The issue – what are the details of the issues in contention? Research the issues and prepare a full and detailed summary of the events that surround it, the documentation and records that support your opinion and those that show that the other party's opinion is flawed. If relevant, obtain independent support for your position from professionals in the relevant field.

- Trade-offs – would you be comfortable accepting some kind of trade-off in order to settle the issues in contention? If so, what do you have to trade that the other party would want, and vice versa?

- Alternatives – what are the alternatives open to you should the negotiations fail? Are you comfortable with these? Know your BATNA (best alternative to negotiated agreement) (see Section 1.1.1). If your BATNA is, for instance, arbitration, do you feel that the issue in contention is worth the expenditure in terms of both time and money that an arbitration would cause you to incur? A risk assessment should be carried out to determine whether it might be more cost-effective, should the negotiations fail, to consider settling for something less than you initially intended, rather than to become embroiled in a lengthy and expensive arbitration hearing, the outcome of which is uncertain. Are the possible advantages of reaching an arbitrated settlement worth the commercial risk?

- Relationships – what is the nature of your relationship with the other party? Assess your relationship with the other party, reviewing any history between you and assessing whether this may or should influence the negotiations in any way. You will need to decide whether you want that relationship to continue after the current contract or whether you are prepared to go all out for a win situation in disregard of the consequences on future relationships. Separate people from the problem; focus on interests not positions.

- Expected outcomes – what are the expected outcomes of the negotiations and how critical are these within the organisations concerned? Promises may have been given which are dependent upon a particular outcome and failure to achieve this might result in loss of face within an organisation or within a community. Are you prepared for this?

- Consequences – what are the consequences of winning or losing on both yourself and the other party? Consider the value of a settlement to your business

rather than the cost. If you are not careful you may run the risk of losing something in the negotiations that is in fact more valuable to your business than money.

- Power – where does the real power lie within your relationship with the other party? What power does the other party have to deliver what you are hoping to achieve from the negotiations? It could be that the issue involves a cost element that the other party just does not have the resources to deliver, in which case your success could be short lived and could result in the other party becoming bankrupt. Your risk assessment should have unearthed this possibility and should have come up with an alternative, lesser solution that would be more acceptable to both parties.

- Possible solutions – what compromises are you prepared to make to resolve the issue?

This list is not exhaustive but it sets a minimum level of preparation and research that needs to be carried out before starting a negotiation. By analysing each of the above items you will not only become more familiar with the issue in dispute and the reasons for your stance, but also with the options available to you should the negotiations veer off track. You will then not be surprised by events as they unfold but will, instead, have the options rehearsed and available to put to the other party, increasing your stature in front of the other party and, with that, your chances of success.

In an ideal world the other party will also have researched the issues in the same way, using a similar checklist to that given above. It will also have reviewed its goals and compromises and you will probably find that your relative positions are not ultimately as fundamentally opposed as they may have initially appeared.

5.7.4 Structure of negotiation meeting

The parties must agree on the structure of the meetings at which the negotiations will take place. This may seem an unnecessary requirement but the structure has great importance. Nothing will be resolved unless the negotiations have a positive structure and are undertaken by suitably empowered representatives of the parties.

If the issue in contention is a complicated one involving commercial and technical issues, then negotiation meetings will need to be structured in such a way that the technical issues can be resolved first, followed by the commercial ones, since the latter will inevitably be dependent upon the former. It is unlikely that the commercial issues would take precedence. The technical issues will probably not require the presence of senior commercial management from either party, and so the initial negotiation team will be composed of the parties' technical representatives. There might also, however, be contractual issues that affect the technical issues, in which case the teams can be enhanced by contract experts from each party as and when required. When the technical issues have been agreed upon the commercial negotiations can begin. Higher management will probably only get involved when the negotiation teams reach a stalemate, or when a final decision has to be reached on a proposed compromise solution.

However the negotiating team is structured it is critical that those sitting at the negotiating table are empowered by their organisation to enter into meaningful negotiations on its behalf. There is nothing so frustrating as getting towards the end of a negotiation meeting only to find that a senior manager joins the discussions and disagrees with everything that has been discussed so far. There must be agreements in place that define how far a particular team can go and at which point more senior members will be required to join the negotiations. These agreements must be made available to all parties to the negotiations so that they are all aware of the limitations of the existing teams, and know when to introduce their own, more senior personnel to the negotiations.

There are different types of negotiator, and all have their place depending upon the particular issues in contention, the opposing party or parties and the goals to be achieved. Examples of the different types are:

- Aggressor – makes attacks on the opposing party's performance, unreasonableness, weakness in its argument, or anything else that can undermine its confidence and imply its case has no substance. In dealing with an aggressive opponent you must stand up for yourself, use assertive language yet avoid direct confrontation.

- Long pauser – listens to the other party but does not respond immediately, appearing to be giving considerable thought to the other party's presentation but secretly hoping that the silence will draw out more information from the other party. In dealing with this type of negotiator you should be patient in waiting for a response and, if no response is forthcoming, tell them what you plan to do.

- Mocking negotiator – mocks and sneers at the other party's proposal in an attempt to undermine its confidence and draw out a response it will later regret. If you meet this type of negotiator just be calm, don't respond aggressively but continue with your presentation in the manner to which you are accustomed.

- Interrogator – meets all proposals with searching questions with the intention of implying that the other party has not prepared well for the negotiation, challenges any answers in a confrontational manner and continues to seek explanations of all further answers. This is where time spent preparing your case will prove to be time well spent, as you should find you have all the answers at your fingertips. If the interrogation introduces arguments that you have not prepared for and that are not totally relevant then discount them as such.

- Reasonable – appears to be reasonable in order to win friends and confidence but meanwhile makes impossible demands. If you meet this type then you should reject all demands that are unreasonable, but do so in a non-threatening manner. Let them know that you value their input and try to find any hidden meaning in their reasonableness.

- Divides and conquers – produces dissention within the other party by forming an alliance with one of the team members at the expense of the others. This causes the other team to have to spend time resolving its own internal conflicts rather than the issue under negotiation. Agreement on team strategies prior to commencement of negotiations should enable you to counter such approaches.

- Acts dumb – pretends to be particularly dense and exasperates the other party in the hope that it will reveal additional information as it tries to find increasingly simple ways of explaining and elaborating on its proposals, or that it concedes points out of pure frustration. In dealing with this type you should raise the question as to why they are so hesitant and, if the negotiation is threatened by such an attitude, ask for their removal from the negotiating team.

5.7.5 Failure of negotiations

Negotiations can fail for a number of reasons, depending upon the issues in contention and the attitudes of the parties to the negotiations. Each party will hopefully have carried out a risk assessment prior to entering into the negotiations and will be aware of the options open to it.

It might well be that one party believes so strongly in its case that it considers it would have a better chance of success if it halted the negotiations and proceeded directly to the next stage provided in the contract. This could be either one of the popular ADR procedures or arbitration. If its risk assessment suggested this prior to the commencement of negotiations then the party would not really have taken much interest in the proceedings, and the negotiations would have been doomed to failure from the outset. The party may, however, have carried out a further risk assessment based upon the information gained during the negotiations and changed its opinion, perhaps as a result of observing weaknesses in the other party's case that were not apparent prior to commencement of the negotiations.

Even if one party refuses to participate in further negotiations, failure of negotiations need not necessarily be fatal. Either party can propose recommencing negotiations (looping back) at any time, although there is obviously not much point in this unless the party has unearthed further evidence that will support its arguments or has reached an agreement internally that allows it to make additional compromises. Even after the ADR or arbitration clauses have been invoked the parties can still, by mutual agreement, revert back to negotiation, so even getting to this stage is not necessarily fatal to the chances of reaching a negotiated settlement.

5.7.6 Reaching an agreement

Hopefully the negotiations will have gone well and the parties will reach agreement on the issues in contention. Once they have reached a final agreement it is important that they put the agreement in writing and that all parties involved sign it. This may seem too obvious an observation to include here but it is surprising how often agreements are made but never confirmed, leaving the door open for further disputes on the same issues later in the contract.

If the terms of the contract require, it might be necessary for the contract to be amended to take account of the settlement agreement. This will require issuance of either an addendum or a variation/change order. It is important to comply precisely with whatever the contract requires in this respect, as to do otherwise could well affect the true value of the settlement agreement.

5.8 ESCALATION AND DE-ESCALATION

5.8.1 Increase in intensity of a dispute

Escalation refers to the increase in both the intensity of a dispute and the severity of the tactics used in pursuing it. Except in special circumstances, such as those described below, escalation of a dispute is best avoided. The more a dispute escalates, the further apart the parties tend to grow and the more intractable they become.

Escalation can come about by a change in company policy concerning the dispute, a change in the personnel involved in negotiating the dispute, or a change in the interaction between the parties. Escalation inevitably results in more personnel becoming involved in the negotiations, encouraging even greater escalation.

Escalation in its extreme forms has five distinct stages:

- Tactics used move from light tactics (persuasion, promises, efforts by one side to please the other) to heavy tactics (threats, power plays).

- The number of issues making up the dispute and the number of people involved in negotiating it increase.

- Issues in dispute move from the specific to the general, and relationships between the disputants deteriorate.

- The number of parties to the dispute increases as more are drawn into the dispute (e.g. a dispute which begins as a dispute between a contractor and a material supplier could escalate to include the subcontractor who was intending to install the materials and the client who was intending to be the end user).

- Goals change from 'reaching a mutually acceptable solution' to 'winning at all costs', even as far as causing some degree of hurt to the other party.

Escalation can be constructive or destructive. This is discussed in more detail below. In many cases the escalation can be tactical in nature and can have positive results, assisting the parties to move towards a settlement that satisfies their respective needs. In other cases the parties are not aware that the dispute is escalating, despite one or other of the disputants being responsible for this happening. The parties guilty of escalation might have been forced into doing so by pressures not necessarily directly related to the dispute (e.g. inter-company policies) and without fully realising the results of their actions or having time to consider the alternatives open to them.

5.8.2 Constructive escalation

Escalation need not necessarily result in an increase in intractability. It is possible to introduce tactics that increase the intensity of the dispute whilst still preventing or limiting intractability.

For example, party A might fear that if the dispute escalates excessively there will be no alternative other than to resort to litigation or arbitration (or whatever the contract prescribes), or even that the contract might be terminated. Party B, even though it might be increasing the intensity of the dispute, perhaps by introducing deadlines for decisions, can defuse the dispute by giving assurances that after the dispute has been settled a mutually satisfactory accommodation will be possible whereby the remainder of the contract can proceed unaffected by the dispute negotiations. Reassurances might also be given that party A's staff will continue to be respected and that their authority will not have been diminished in any way by the fact that they have reached a compromise settlement on the dispute in question.

The introduction of persuasive practices might be seen as escalating the dispute, but can again contribute to an early settlement by containing the dispute within strict boundaries and limiting the destructive tendencies that might otherwise creep in. Party A could suggest that if settlement is reached within a set period of time party B would benefit in some way, possibly by receiving payment of the monies agreed under the settlement within a shorter period of time than required under the contract. The fact that party A is setting a deadline for reaching settlement could be viewed as escalating the dispute. However, this escalation is constructive since it uses persuasion, in the form of the promise of early payment, to make settlement attractive to party B.

5.8.3 Destructive escalation

Escalation can also occur as a result of preconceived impressions one party has about the other. For example, one party may have been left feeling aggrieved by the other in past dealings. In such a situation the aggrieved party would tend to over-react to anything the other party said that it disagreed with, even though its reason for feeling aggrieved, and therefore the resultant escalation, had nothing to do with the dispute in question. Hostility-driven disputes such as this tend to provoke new disputes and the aggrieved party can come to view revenge for past actions as the desired result. This is a typical example of destructive escalation, a situation that should not be allowed to happen.

In a typical aggressor–defender model, the aggressor party is perceived by the defender party as having a goal that is in direct contradiction to the goal of the defender. The mild approach taken by the aggressor at the outset of negotiations quickly changes to a harder approach and the defender responds in a similar manner at each change in tactic by the aggressor. This reactive escalation of the dispute has destructive results as the parties grow further and further apart.

The previous example relates to an escalation that moved in one direction only. An equally common model is where the escalation moves in a spiral caused by a circular motion of action and reaction. Each reaction tends to be more intense and severe than the preceding action as new issues or grievances are introduced into the dispute. Tactics change from light to heavy and the issues in dispute grow, causing both parties concern that there is no end in sight.

This type of destructive escalation can be retaliatory or defensive. The retaliatory model is where each party punishes the other in response to actions that left it feeling aggrieved. The defensive model is where a party responds according to preconceived impressions, perhaps due to past dealings with the other party, that cause it to be wary in its responses.

In other dispute situations the tactics employed by one party in fighting the dispute precipitate changes in the approach of the opposing party. This results in the parties forgetting about the initial issues in dispute and instead concentrating on basic principles. The parties' intentions change from attempting to reach an amicable settlement to winning at all costs. This kind of destructive escalation is common where the dispute negotiations are handled by personnel who have been involved in the issues in dispute from its outset. If this is to be avoided the dispute has to be handed up to more senior staff who are less influenced by past events than the facts of the case.

5.8.4 Understand threats of escalation

Disputes can escalate without the parties being aware that this is happening. By the time that they eventually become aware of the escalation it is often too late to eliminate fully the damage that it has caused.

It is important that all project staff have been trained to recognise escalation. They must know to report it immediately to senior management so that the necessary strategies can be devised in order to reduce the damage. Training should be directed initially at identifying changes in the tone of both written and verbal communications and also changes in the body language of the other party's representatives.

It might be that at the outset of the dispute, negotiation meetings were being held on a regular basis, and that the meetings were attended by senior personnel from all the parties. If arranged meetings start to be cancelled, or if the period between meetings becomes extended at the request of the other party, or if the other party starts sending junior personnel to represent it at the meetings, these will be warning signs that the other party has lost interest in resolving the dispute by negotiation. Unless the other party is considering withdrawing from the dispute, this loss of interest will result in an escalation since the only way forward will be to adopt whatever formal dispute resolution procedures are required under the particular contract.

A further sign of escalation, probably more easily identifiable to the untrained eye, would be if more senior members of the other party's management started attending the negotiating meetings. The procedures may also become more formal, with increased record taking and reporting of the negotiations to all concerned. A more serious sign of escalation would be when the other party starts involving external specialist consultants and lawyers in the meeting, and when written communications come from these external specialists rather than from the other party's own staff.

Staff can be trained to identify these and other relevant changes, and must take immediate steps to include senior management in all future discussions, particularly as regards the strategies to be adopted in the negotiation meetings and subsequent correspondence.

5.8.5 Ground rules reduce chance of escalation

When contentious issues are recognised as becoming disputes and the parties agree to commence negotiations it is prudent to establish rules under which the negotiations will be carried out. This has been discussed in earlier sections, where it was suggested that an MOU setting out the parties' expectations should be agreed before negotiations commence. This could be extended to include procedural rules such as:

* who will represent the parties at the negotiations – seniority grades, disciplines and numbers;
* at what stage (and who will decide) should these representatives be replaced with more senior management;
* the frequency of negotiation meetings;
* the optimum amount of time to be allowed for each meeting;
* at what stage should a break be called to allow a period for reflection;

- at what stage should the negotiations be deemed failed and decisions made as to whether the next step in dispute resolution should commence.

5.8.6 Cooling off periods

If a party has reason to believe that the dispute has started escalating and is uncomfortable with this then it would be advised to propose that the parties enter into a cooling off period. This gives each party the opportunity of reviewing where it now stands as regards the issues in dispute, how successful the negotiations have been so far, and how its representatives and those of the other parties have performed.

The cooling off period must be put to good use. It is of no use to anyone merely to walk away from the negotiating table for three or four weeks. Those weeks must be used to carry out a thorough review of all aspects of the dispute and the negotiations. This is a period when each party can review and, if it deems appropriate after studying the results of its review, revise its strategies. Each management team can use this time to decide whether the present negotiating team should be retained for the next phase of negotiations or whether it would be better to replace it with a fresh team. If the strategy is to be changed then it might be advisable to change the negotiating team. This would not only reduce the chances of the old team being reluctant to implement the new strategy with the same enthusiasm, but would also give a clear indication to the other party that a fresh approach is being introduced in an effort to reach a reasonable settlement.

5.8.7 Reduction in intensity of escalation

One way to reduce the intensity of a dispute to head off escalation is to change the parties' representatives at the negotiating table. The existing members may have become stale and may be on the verge of polarising their positions. That, if it were allowed to happen, would seriously undermine the objectives of dispute resolution.

If one party can see that the other party is escalating the dispute then it should draw its attention to the likely consequences. Fear of the consequences of escalation can often bring the parties back down to earth and encourage them to work harder to build a settlement. Disputes are less likely to escalate out of control if the parties are aware of the consequences.

5.8.8 De-escalation

When a dispute has reached a significantly high level of intensity the parties must resort to de-escalation strategies such as those mentioned below in order to overcome the increasing escalation and make progress towards finding a solution to the dispute. Movement from escalation to de-escalation should be a gradual and systematic process, taking whatever measures are deemed appropriate for the particular case.

De-escalation usually comes after the parties have reached a productive stalemate and their representatives cannot envisage any developments that will move the dispute forward. The point of maximum conflict intensity and destructiveness has then been reached, and a reassessment of the situation is called for. De-escalation is a much more difficult process to implement than escalation and usually starts with a gradual reduction in tensions through reciprocal gestures between the parties. The parties will hopefully determine that their current strategies will not succeed, and they will start developing new ways of thinking with the intention of de-escalating the dispute and reaching a resolution acceptable to all.

De-escalation will require one party to make a small conciliatory gesture that the other party can then reciprocate to. For example, party A might decide the time is ripe to appoint new representatives either in place of or in addition to its previous representatives. If party B does not respond with a similar change of representative then a further conciliatory gesture may be made in such a way that party B is left in no doubt of party A's willingness to de-escalate the dispute. Once the desired reciprocation has been given, a larger, more important conciliatory gesture can be made. If this is similarly reciprocated then a spiral of conciliatory de-escalation will have been initiated, taking the place of the escalation cycle that would otherwise have spiralled out of control.

5.8.9 De-escalation strategies

The principal de-escalation strategies that should be considered for application, depending upon the nature of the dispute and the degree of escalation that has occurred, are as follows:

- **Opening new channels of communication**
  It may well be that the current representatives of the parties in dispute have gone as far as they can go, or are empowered to go. A new line of communication should be introduced, possibly at head office level in place of site level.

- **Suspension of any sanctions already imposed**
  Sanctions might have been imposed by one party upon the other in order to 'encourage' it to settle. Such sanctions might include withholding monies otherwise due, restricting access to sections of work yet to be commenced or delaying authorisation of dayworks, invoices etc. Their removal would show a spirit of cooperation that might not have been previously apparent.

- **Removal of intransigent or negative dispute management leadership**
  The dispute team might be functioning reasonably well, but might be prevented from reaching a settlement by one dominant person who is reluctant to back down on a particular issue. The rest of the team, or a more flexible replacement leader, might be able to reach a settlement following the removal of this one obstacle.

- **Acknowledgement of some responsibility for the dispute**
  It is more than likely that each party has some degree of responsibility in relation to the issue in dispute. This need not necessarily mean that each party is responsible for the actual issue in dispute (although this might well be the case) but each might have some responsibility for allowing it to reach the dispute stage. It could be that one party should have brought the issue to the other party's attention earlier, when it could have been resolved without reaching the dispute stage, and that the other party is aware of and is taking issue on it. This needs to be acknowledged so that the parties can move their negotiations on to the real substance of the dispute.

- **Recognition of the existence and possible legitimacy of the other party's stance**
  Often one party fails to recognise that the other party's opinion has any worth, where in all probability it has, albeit not necessarily to the degree that would be necessary for it to win the argument. It still, however, needs to be recognised by the other party and given due consideration in the negotiations.

- **Separation of the dispute into individual and distinct issues**
  If the dispute can be divided into several individual and distinct issues then it might be possible to discuss each issue on its own merits without reference to the other associated issues. If a solution can be found to each of the parts then it gives the parties encouragement that a solution to the whole may in fact be possible. This in turn will encourage the parties to continue with the negotiations in a conciliatory manner in an effort to find a solution.

- **Participation in informal discussions aimed at finding solutions to the issues in dispute**
  If the formal dispute negotiations are not going anywhere the dispute may be in danger of escalating further. At this point it might be prudent to consider entering into less formal negotiations. 'Off the record' discussions, possibly on neutral territory, could help the parties to find common ground, which could kick start further formal negotiations and lead to a settlement.

5.8.10 Develop personal relationships

People who have a personal relationship are more likely to communicate effectively and understand each other's intentions than those who do not. It cannot be emphasised enough that the most effective and simplest way to avoid disputes escalating out of control is to have built good personal relationships with your opposite number and the opposing team before the dispute was identified. This may be done in a planned way, such as by organising participant events such as football matches, paintball games and other so-called 'bonding' events. However, the best way is to bring the people concerned together in a relaxed and informal way. This could be on a one-to-one basis over a meal or a drink, or could involve mixing as families. Basically, anything is better than nothing, and the less strained the get-togethers are the better will be the responses of the parties, the more likely such get-togethers are to happen again, and the more likely they are to benefit the parties and the project.

Care must be taken to ensure that these get-togethers could not in any way be interpreted as intended to compromise the other party's position in any current or potential disputes. For this reason the costs of all entertainment should either be shared at the time or reciprocated shortly after, and higher-level management should be kept aware of what is happening and to what extent relationships have developed. They might well consider at some point that the relationship has become too close and that it could have detrimental effects on the project, at which time they might decide to separate the parties as far as business is concerned.

5.8.11 Dealing with destructive speech

Destructive speech is a major contributory factor to the escalation of disputes. Often it involves the use of provocative statements, some of which might have been said unintentionally or with a lack of knowledge of how they would be taken by the opposing party. Particular destructive speech issues occur when dealing in international environments, where the parties concerned might be of different nationalities and come from different cultural and religious backgrounds. Statements made by one party using words that are in common usage in its home country might have a totally different meaning to the other party due to cultural or religious connotations.

In an international context there is also room for misunderstanding what was actually said from a purely linguistic viewpoint. What was intended as a simple statement of fact can easily be interpreted as a provocative statement merely because of a mistranslation of an otherwise innocuous word or phrase.

Destructive speech cannot really be dealt with after the event. It can be explained away as a misunderstanding, if in fact that is what it was, but the other party might be convinced that this is a tactical withdrawal and that the actual statement was the true intent of the party making it. In order to avoid destructive speech the parties should understand clearly what they are going to say at the negotiating table. They should also take whatever measures are appropriate to ensure that the other party is able to understand its intention. If there is the least chance of a misunderstanding due to language difficulties then it would be wise to produce a written summary of the basic facts being put forward to the negotiations, and to have this translated in to whatever language or languages the other parties are familiar with.

5.8.12 Controlled confrontation

Confrontation in a dispute context is a self-conscious and bi-directional process of power play and testing, constantly escalating and de-escalating as negotiations progress.

Parties to a dispute must develop ways in which escalation can be allowed to develop whilst ensuring that they can prevent it running away in a destructive manner. Where the dispute concerns several issues, or the issue in dispute has several facets, it would be an advantage if the negotiating team could limit discussions to one issue or facet at a time. This will decrease the likelihood of the overall dispute running out of control.

The leaders of the opposing negotiation teams must make every effort to maintain cordial relationships between their teams. They must also ensure that distortion of information transferred from one party to the other is minimised by open discussion between the team leaders at all stages of the dispute negotiations.

Where control is still found to be difficult it may be possible, depending upon the exact nature of the dispute, to persuade the other party that the negotiations represent a joint effort and that both parties will ultimately benefit if a mutually agreeable solution is found. In this way it may be possible to dilute any aggression and channel it into positive action aimed at resolving the issues in dispute.

5.8.13 Changing leaders

When a dispute has been going on for some time, and negotiations are either in a stalemate situation or are escalating out of control, the parties have to take action to prevent it becoming an intractable dispute.

One of the first steps to take is to change the negotiating team leader. It is inevitable that after a period of time the initial team leader will come to believe that a particular line of argument is the only one that has any relevance to the dispute. A fresh face might come up with a different argument altogether, or may simply be perceived by the opposing party to be of a more amenable disposition and a person that they can do business with.

The initial team leaders will probably have been appointed at an early stage in the dispute, when the parties were not fully aware of the particular attributes of the opposing party's negotiation team members. After a period of negotiation they will be more aware of the qualities, both good and bad, of their opponent's team and of the strengths of their arguments. They will be in a stronger position to select leaders who will be able to put forward their arguments in a manner more appropriate to the situation as it is perceived at that point in time.

5.8.14 Crisis management

Crisis management is not the ideal way to avoid or resolve disputes. However, it is sometimes necessary due to the particular circumstances encountered. Crisis management mechanisms should be discussed and planned in case the need arises; by its very definition, when a crisis does occur, management needs to act promptly to resolve it. Crisis management mechanisms should be designed to help the parties deal with dispute situations that are escalating and which are putting pressure on the parties to reach an agreement without having due time to consider the options available to them. No agreement should be reached without giving due consideration to all options. The crisis management machinery should allow for this, possibly introducing the ability to reach interim agreements where these would be appropriate in order that work can continue while crisis discussions are concluded. In this way escalation is controlled and is not allowed to damage the relationship between the parties.

5.8.15 Focus on future relationships

Escalation can sometimes be restrained by encouraging the parties to focus on the continuation of relationships between them. Emphasis should be placed on the fact that they would like to maintain and build on past relationships, thereby taking the focus off the assignment of blame and punishment.

This only applies where a future relationship is both possible and desired by each of the parties. It might be that one party has no intention of continuing the relationship, perhaps because it is pulling out of the particular market or area concerned or because it does not feel comfortable with the relationship it has experienced. In such a case other measures will have to be put into play in order to minimise escalation of the dispute.

5.8.16 Achieve settlement of dispute

In a dispute situation the main objective of the parties must be to settle at the earliest opportunity. This will necessarily require a cessation of escalation and an acceleration of de-escalation. All the tactics and strategies mentioned in this section have a part to play in this process, and it is up to the parties to determine which are most suitable for the particular dispute in question. Despite using all the tactics at their disposal, a settlement might not be reached. At this point the parties must decide what their alternatives are, whether this means mediation, adjudication, arbitration or litigation. They may determine, however, that the dispute is too small to warrant the added expense of taking one of these routes. Alternatively, one of the parties might feel that its arguments are not robust enough to withstand the rigours of independent scrutiny and that it is time to negotiate in earnest in order to achieve a settlement.

5.9 ALTERNATIVE DISPUTE RESOLUTION

Alternative dispute resolution (ADR) is a term that covers a variety of different ways of facilitating the resolution of disputes without recourse to the courts. It can involve different processes and can be triggered by different events in different countries. There are various ADR mechanisms available, including mediation, conciliation, adjudication, expert determination, early neutral evaluation and mini-trials. In the context of this section, arbitration is excluded as an ADR mechanism because although it is technically an alternative to litigation it has many characteristics that are similar to litigation, making it a parallel process rather than an alternative one.

ADR has several advantages over litigation or arbitration as a means of resolving construction disputes. ADR is considered to be:

- less expensive;

- potentially quicker;

- kinder to the long-term relationships between the parties;

- instrumental in enhancing communication between the parties;

- as private as the parties desire it to be;

- non-binding on the parties until a settlement is agreed;

- a means to preserve the parties' legal rights and available processes until a final settlement is agreed;

- concerned with the settlement of the dispute only;

- an option that is available at any stage of the contract or the dispute;

- a procedure that enables the parties' principals to participate to a greater extent in the early resolution of the dispute.

On the minus side, ADR can have the following disadvantages:

- a final solution is not a guaranteed end result as either party can abandon the mechanism at any time;

- a higher degree of openness than a party may be prepared to conform to may be necessary in order to progress the process;

- the end result does not provide a precedent which can be applied to later similar disputes on the same or different projects or by third parties in similar disputes;

- each party must consent to the process and must cooperate fully in the process in a consensual rather than an adversarial way.

For further details regarding the strengths and weaknesses of the various methods of ADR and more detailed descriptions of the various ADR mechanisms mentioned above the reader should refer to *International Construction Contract Management*, written by the author of this book and also published by RIBA Publishing (ISBN 978 1 85946 169 3).

CHAPTER 5 SUMMARY

1. The way in which a potential dispute is dealt with initially has a significant influence on how costly the process will ultimately be, and so it is important to map the dispute out at the earliest opportunity.

2. Dispute avoidance involves in part reversing the dynamics that caused the issues to come into contention and changing them into dynamics of resolution.

3. Analyse the issues which are causing concern and which have the potential to escalate into disputes. You may find that you agree with the other party on a number of issues. You can then de-emphasise the areas of potential dispute and emphasise the areas of agreement.

4. Reach a formal agreement on the issues in dispute prior to commencement of negotiations so that each party is aware of exactly what the issues are.

5. It is important that each dispute be dealt with in an impersonal manner.

6. Dispute negotiations should be based upon the documentation exchanged by the parties, rather than merely being based on preconceived ideas and opinions.

7. The other party's views should be considered with respect.

continued. . .

8. Avoid maintaining your position without considering the developing situation and how this would affect both your company's and the project's best interests.

9. Prepare a summary at the end of each round of negotiations confirming any agreements reached and any changes to the issues in contention, so that each party is clear as to where they stand before proceeding further.

10. It may be sensible for a party to make a judgment that an issue is not of sufficient importance, or does not have sufficient impact, to justify the costs of confrontation.

11. Negotiation is an interactive process undertaken in an attempt to reach agreement through discussions on an issue or issues upon which there is currently disagreement.

12. Have confidence in your ability to negotiate your way to success and keep control of the negotiations at all times.

13. Separate people from the problem: focus on interests not positions.

14. Nothing will be resolved unless the negotiations have a positive structure and are undertaken by suitably empowered representatives of the parties.

15. Escalation (the increase in intensity of a dispute) can come about by a change in company policy concerning the dispute, a change in the personnel involved in negotiating the dispute, or a change in the interaction between the parties.

16. If the dispute can be seen to be escalating, the parties should enter into a cooling off period to give each of them the opportunity to review where they stand as regards the issues in dispute and the progress made so far.

17. Movement from escalation to de-escalation should be a gradual and systematic process, taking whatever measures are deemed appropriate in the sequence that best suits the evolution of the particular case.

18. The most effective and simplest way to avoid disputes escalating out of control is to build good personal relationships with your opposite number and with the opposing team.

19. People who have a personal relationship are more likely to communicate effectively and understand each other's intentions than those who do not.

Index

NB page numbers in **bold** refer to text in figures.

Index